PLANES and PILOTS

THE CURTISS
P-40

From 1939 to 1945

Anis EL BIED
Daniel LAURELUT
Translated from the French by Alan McKay

HISTOIRE & COLLECTIONS

SOLID and EVER PRESENT

The story of the P-40 is closely linked to the difficulties that faced the Allies confronting the Axis powers at the beginning of the war. Although it was never an exceptional thoroughbred aircraft like the P-51 for instance, in the West the P-40 is remembered as one of America's most numerous and reliable fighters; in the East it was the destroyer of the Zero - a reputation carefully orchestrated by American propaganda and the statements of certain pilots - with Claire Lee Chennault's famous Flying Tigers in 1941-42. Although the P-40 never actually faced the Zero over China and Burma, the Zero was far better for its reputation than were the Claudes, the Hayabusas and the twin-engined planes which were its daily lot. When the United States entered the war following the attack on Pearl Harbor on 7 December 1941, the P-40 was the mainstay of the US Army Air Force. These machines - P-36s and P-40B/Cs - lined up on Wheeler and Bellows Fields without fuel and ammunition, inauspiciously inaugurated the fighter's career in American colours by getting shot up on the ground by the Japanese.

Its strong and reliable airframe, driven by an Allison engine which was also used on the P-39 and P-38, had originally been designed to take a radial engine which had already been mounted on its immediate forerunners, the P-36 and H-75 and did not change very much as far as its general silhouette was concerned until the end of the war when the last experiments tried to make an exceptional fighter out of it, at a time when the Curtiss firm was running out of ideas and a lot of its projects were coming to nothing.

The P-40 was a combination of both elegant and squat lines which gave it that peculiar look which its large intake did nothing to improve. It was a «man's» plane, needing a firm hand when taxiing while the tailwheel was still on the ground, a careful watch on the flight path with the rudder bar - sometimes the pilot literally had to stand on the left-hand pedal at high speeds (it was said that you could recognise a P-40 pilot by the size of his thighs!), a good hold of the joystick when climbing as the plane had a natural and very pronounced tendency to dive and accelerate which was not made up for by the heaviness of its elevators. It could easily be out-climbed as its Allison engine did not have the necessary intake power that a two-stage compressor would have given it. Its ailerons were very sensitive and held the airstream very well and although faced with opponents who had the advantage in other areas, the P-40 was thus able to get inside their turning circle quickly and find a favourable position to fire from.

The plane's design and the choice of powerplant, which was to handicap the full development potential of its airframe, originated at the beginning of the thirties when those responsible for the

(©ECPAD/France)

defence of North America tended to favour the development of long-range bombers, fighters being relegated to the ground attack and coastal protection roles. As a result, it was decided to develop a robust machine, powered first by a radial engine, then by the Allison V-1710 in-line engine which was good at low altitudes but notoriously inefficient above 15 000 feet. A similar decision limited the potential of other aircraft like the P-39 which was otherwise a particularly modern aircraft although it never saw front line service, at least with the Anglo-Americans; the Russians seem to have been more than satisfied with its capabilities.

Be that as it may, 13 700 P-40s were turned out during the war, production only stopping on 30 November 1944. Apart from Amer-

Official handing over ceremony of P-40Fs to the GC II/5 of Commandant Rozanoff at Alger-Maison Blanche in January 1943.

ican squadrons, the RAF and the Commonwealth air forces (Australia, Canada, South Africa, New-Zealand) received 2 800 machines together with other countries like China, the USSR - which received 2 070 machines under the Lend-Lease Agreement like the other Allied countries, France and Brazil or Turkey.

NB. The different designations given to the P-40 can sometimes be confusing as the H and the P were often applied to the same plane. The official designation for the Curtiss factory began with an H (H-75, H-81). When delivered to the USAAC, the planes became the P-36 and the P-40, P being used for Pursuit - fighter.

A P-40F, G.C. II/5 Lafayette being rearmed in North Africa, 1943. This version is recognisable by the absence of the long air intake above the engine cowling. (© ECPAD/France)

Kittyhawk of No 112 Squadron RAF in North Africa. It was this RAF squadron, not the Flying Tigers of the AVG in China, as has been popularly and incorrectly supposed, who invented the famous shark's teeth. (IWM)

5

CURTISS P-40'S NOSE ART and UNITS INSIGNIA

CURTISS P-40'S NOSE ART and UNITS INSIGNIA

25 "STAR DUST"

26

27

28

29

30 "Texas Longhorn"

31

32 TRIXIE

33 Joyce

34 RR

35 H.H.G

36 B

37 "POP"

38

39 SAWTOOTH

40 Lighthouse Louie

41 Gerry

42 STUD

43

44

45

46 Geronimo!

47

48

49 KAY THE STRAWBERRY BLONDE

CURTISS P-40'S NOSE ART and UNITS INSIGNIA

1. Insignia of the Flying Tigers specially drawn by Disney for the AVG. This was supplied as a decal which was applied directly onto the fuselage protected by a layer of varnish.

2. The «Adam and Eve» insignia worn by the P-40 B/Cs of the 1st Pursuit Squadron of the AVG.

3. Insignia worn by the P-40 B/C of the 2nd Pursuit squadron (together with that of the panda not shown here) of the AVG.

4. The red angel of the P-40B/Cs existed in different poses as shown by these five illustrations.

5. Another variant of the famous AVG Tiger, shown here with a Chinese roundel as background with a Japanese flag in shreds.

6. Insignia of the 33rd Pursuit Squadron, seen on a P-40C in 1941 in the USA.

7. Insignia applied to P-40Cs in the 55th Pursuit Squadron (20th Pursuit Group) in service in the USA at the beginning of the fighter's career.

8. Scorpion of the 64th Fighter Squadron (57th Fighter Group) called the «Black Scorpions» equipped with P-40Fs, North Africa, 1943.

9. Egyptian falcon in a cartouche painted on «Little Joe», a P-40F of the 79th Fighter Group flown by Col. Earl E. Bates, North Africa, 1943.

10 &13. Insignia painted under the exhaust pipes and in front of the country roundel of P-40K n° 255 white of Major Edward M. Nolmeyer, 26th Fighter Squadron, 51st Fighter group, Kunming, China, December 1943.

11. Tiger's head of the P-40E of the 11th Fighter Squadron, 343rd Fighter Group, based at Kiska in the Aleutian Islands.

12. Insignia applied to a P-40L piloted by Col. William K. Sandy McNown of the 324th Fighter Group, Ceco-la Italy, December 1943.

14 & 16. Insignia of the 79th Pursuit Squadron and the 20th Pursuit Group applied under the exhaust pipes and the rudder of a P-40 E which had taken part in military exercises in the USA in 1941.

15. Parrot's head painted on the front of P-40N used for advanced pilot training at Napier Fields, Alabama, November 1943.

17. Insignia of the 7th Fighter Squadron, 49th Fighter Group seen on a P-40 E piloted by Captain William J. Hennon, Darwen, Australia, 1942.

18. Insignia showing a mosquito carrying a bomb seen on a P-40 E of the 11th Fighter squadron, 343rd Fighter Group based at Adak in Alaska in September 1942.

19. This bird was seen painted on a P-40F of the 65th Fighter Squadron, 57th Fighter Group in North Africa, 1943.

20. Insignia surmounted by «Lee's Hope» appearing on the front of a P-40F of the 85th Fighter Squadron, 79th Fighter Group, flown by Lt Robert J. Duffield at Capodichino in Italy, February 1944.

21. No doubt one of the more interesting insignias worn by P-40s, thanks to the artistic skills of Sergeant Pumphrey attached to the 86th Fighter Squadron, 79th Fighter Group equipped with P-40 F/Ls.

22. Insignia of a P-40F piloted by Lt Paul G. McArthur of the 87th Fighter Squadron, 79th Fighter Group, at Hani West in Tunisia, 1943.

23. Sioux's head of the Lafayette Squadron seen on the H-75s engaged in the Battle of France and on the P-40Fs of the GCII/5 officially delivered on 8 January 1943 in Algiers in the presence of Commandant Rozannof, the unit's commanding officer.

24. One of the numerous drawings adopted to represent the famous skulls used by the P-40Ns of the 80th Fighter Group, based in India in 1943-44. This group's distinctive insignia was introduced by Lt Freeling «Dixie» Clower of the 89th Fighter Squadron.

25. «Stars and Dust» featured on the front of a P-40 flown by Lt Andrew J. Reynolds of the 9th Fighter Squadron, 49th Fighter Group, Darwin, Australia, 1942. This very well-known plane which has been the subject of a lot of models, was also painted with a black and white bird of prey just in front of the country roundel.

26. Death's head with a Tomahawk seen on a P-40 E of the 9th Fighter Squadron, 49th Fighter Group, summer 1942, flown by Lt. Clay Tice.

27. Woman's portrait on a white and blue background seen on a P-40 E of the 9th Fighter Squadron, 49th Fighter Group, Darwin, Australia, 1942, flown by John Landers.

28. A shot of a P-40 E of the 9th Fighter Squadron, 49th Fighter Group, Darwin, Australia, 1942, the masking indicating that the plane was originally assigned to the RAAF, flown by Lt Bob Vaught.

29. «Typhoon McGoon» was the name given later to this cartoon monkey, who originally did not have a name, on one of the P-40 E of the 7th Fighter Squadron, 49th Fighter Group flown by Lt Clyde V. Kinsley.

30. «Texas Longhorn» was one of best known nose art paintings used by the P-40s, here an E of the 9th Fighter Squadron, 49th Fighter Group, Rorona, New Guinea, 1942, flown by Lt John Landers.

31. White eagle used by a P-40E of the 18th Fighter Squadron, 343rd Fighter Group at Alexai Point Field, Adak Ismand in the Aleutian Islands, 1942.

32. Rather interestingly elaborate nose art painted on a P-40L of the 318th Fighter Squadron, 325th Fighter Group, piloted by Capt. Joseph D. Bloomer, commanding the unit at Mateur, Tunisia, autumn 1943.

33. The inscription «Joyce» appeared over the exhaust pipes of a P-40F of an unidentified training unit.

34. This Gothic «KK» was seen on the front of an unpainted P-40F from an unidentified unit, Italy 1943.

35. This stylised « H.H.G.» with a claw on a white background was painted on the front of a P-40F and represented the initials of Lt Hershey H «Herky»

Green, 317th Fighter Squadron, 325th Fighter Group, Mateur, Tunisia, summer 1943.

36. This «B» run through by an arrow was painted on the rudder of a P-40K of the 25th Fighter Squadron, 51st Fighter Group, based at Yunnanyi in China during the summer of 1944. Flown by Charles J. White.

37. «Pop» painted on the front of a P-40K of the 66th Fighter Squadron, 57th Fighter Group, Cap Bon, Tunisia, May 1943.

38. This pin up was painted on a dark background probably green, on a P-40L, flown by Capt. Bruce E. Hunt of the 314th Fighter Squadron, 324th Fighter Group, Cercola, Italy, November 1942.

39. «Sawtooth», a horse painted on a blue and green backdrop, preceded by the inscription «Apache»was the distinctive mark of a P-40L of the 317th Fighter Squadron, 325th Fighter Group, flown by Flt. Off. Cecil O. Dean, Mateur, Tunisia May 1943.

40. «Lighthouse Louie», a broken lighthouse was the distinctive insignia of a P-40L of the 317th Fighter Squadron, 325th Fighter Group, who specialised in attacks on that type of objective, flown by Lt Col Gordon H. Austin, Tunisia, 1943.

41. «Gerry» worn by a P-40L flown by Lt Ralph L. Griffith of the 58th Fighter Squadron, 33rd Fighter Group, Naples, Italy, beginning of 1944.

42. This is very famous nose art, this «Stud» with the Ace of Spades appeared on an all-black P-40F flown by Lt Col Robert Baseler, commanding officer of the 325th Fighter Group, Mateur, Tunisia, autumn 1943.

43. Cowboy on the Japanese Rising Sun, on a P-40 E of the 16th Fighter Squadron, 23rd Fighter Group, China, 1942.

44. This small sized skull was found under the cockpit of a P-40K of the 64th Fighter Squadron, 57th Fighter Group at Hain Main, Tunisia, 1943, with the Scorpion already seen on profile No 8 at the front, under the exhaust pipes.

45. A pink orchid painted on the front of a P-40N of the 7th Fighter Squadron, 49th Fighter Group flown by Robert de Haven, New Guinea, 1943.

46. « Geronimo» was another elaborate painting used on a P-40N of the 45th Fighter Squadron, 15th Fighter Group in the Nanumea Islands in December 1943, flown by Lt Bruce Campbell.

47. A rather famous insignia, if only because taken up by a lot of models, this death's head wearing a helmet was seen on P-40N of the 7th Fighter Squadron, 49th Fighter Group, flown by Lt Joel B. Paris, Philippine Islands, 1944.

48. This unidentified insignia was found behind the country roundel (white star on a blue background without stripes) of a P-40L, from a training unit, C. 1943.

49. «Kay, he Strawberry Blonde» was worn by the P-40 E/Ns of the 8th Fighter Squadron (49th Fighter Group) commanded by Lt Sammy Pierce.

NB. Most of the P-40 insignias appear in the aircraft profiles presented in this work.

"SHARKMOUTH"

 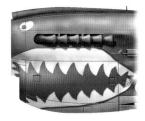  

One of the principal features of the P-40 was
the «Sharkmooth» painted on the air intake and made famous
by the «Flying Tigers». Here is a selection of those found
on almost every version of the fighter during the Second World
War. Most of the Shark's Teeth variants appear
in the profiles in this book and may be consulted in order
to check on the unit and the version. The only exception
is the White Skull painted on the front of the P-40Ns
of the 80th Fighter Group in India in 1943-44.
There is an original specimen on the far left of the second
last row which shows only the jaw after the top had been
taken off when a panel was changed.

Aleutians Islands

Canada

Iceland

Great Britain

France

United-States

323736

Atlantic Ocean

North Afica

114 315

Pacific Ocean

RENEE

Hawaii

10

Panama

29985

JI

Brazil

Atlantic Ocean

Pacific Ocean

CURTISS P-40 at WAR
(Operations Theatres and users)

USSR

India

Burma

China

Japan

Pacific
Ocean

Central
Pacific

New
Guinea

*Inadian
Ocean*

South
Africa

Australia

New-
Zealand

South
Pacific

11

The CURTISS P-36 and H-75

It is difficult to talk about the P-40 without mentioning the H-75 which it resembled for a long time.

The monoplane era really started in America with the P-26 Pea Shooter which was flown as early as March 1932. In Europe, research units brought out refined high-performance fighters like the Me 109 in Germany, the Spitfire in England and to a lesser degree the Morane 406 in France. In the United States, a replacement for the P-26 was required, capable of reaching the 300 mph barrier. It had also to be of all-metal construction (except for the canvas parts of the wings and the tailplane), with a low wing and good performance, especially where rate of climb and manoeuvrability were concerned; it was to be equipped with a radial engine and at least two machine guns.

Prototype tests took place in May 1935 during a competition in which Consolidated, Northrop and Seversky also took part.

Studies began in November 1934 under Donovan R. Berlin who had just joined Curtiss. The first prototype of the Model 75 first flew in April 1935. It was powered by a Wright XR-1670 radial rated at 900 bhp. Engine problems delayed the final evaluation and when this had been carried out, Curtis was awarded a contract for three Y1 P-36 prototypes (official factory designation: H-75 E) on 7 August 1936, even though Seversky, with its P-35, had also been awarded a contract for 77 machines.

Delivered between February and March 1937, these three prototypes (registered under 37-068, 69 and 70) equipped with a Pratt and Whitney R-1830-13 rated at 1050 bhp at full throttle, won the last com-

A Norwegian Curtiss H-75 A8 painted pale green with black letters and the colours of the country on the tail. After the country's invasion by the Wehrmacht, these planes which had actually been delivered were transferred to a training centre in Canada called «Little Norway». *(MAP)*

petition against improved versions of the P-35 in June 1937, and enabled Curtiss to win an order for 210 P-36s or H-75Ls (178As were delivered followed by 32 P-36Cs equipped with two extra machine guns following a decision taken in January 1939) for a total amount of $ 4 113 550.

Delivery started at Wright Field in April 1938 and trouble started immediately: exhaust and wing surface problems which substantially increased the fighter's weight (which went up from 2485 to 2570kg) and reduced its top speed - which went from 315 mph (504kph) to 302 mph (483kph) - when they were solved. As it was manoeuvrable, sound, pleasant to fly and easy to maintain, the authorities were satisfied.

It was delivered to the US Army Air Corps Pursuit Groups based in the United states and abroad (Hawaii, Puerto Rico, Panama) and offered for sale from 1937 to countries as different as Argentina, Siam, China, Brazil, Norway, Holland, Finland, Peru, India, South Africa, Portugal, France and Great Britain with all sorts of modifications to the undercarriage, armament and powerplants. Slightly fewer than 1 000 (including the prototypes) P-36 or Hawk 75s were produced and the design was in fact at the origin of some of the powerplant and armament problems which were to plague production of the P-40.

Curtiss H-75 C1 N° 208 of the GC II/5 Lafayette (3ᵉ Escadrille). After the Armistice, this unit was given the task of defending the big African towns, Oran, Casablanca, Dakar. (Musée de l'Air)

CURTISS P-36/H-75

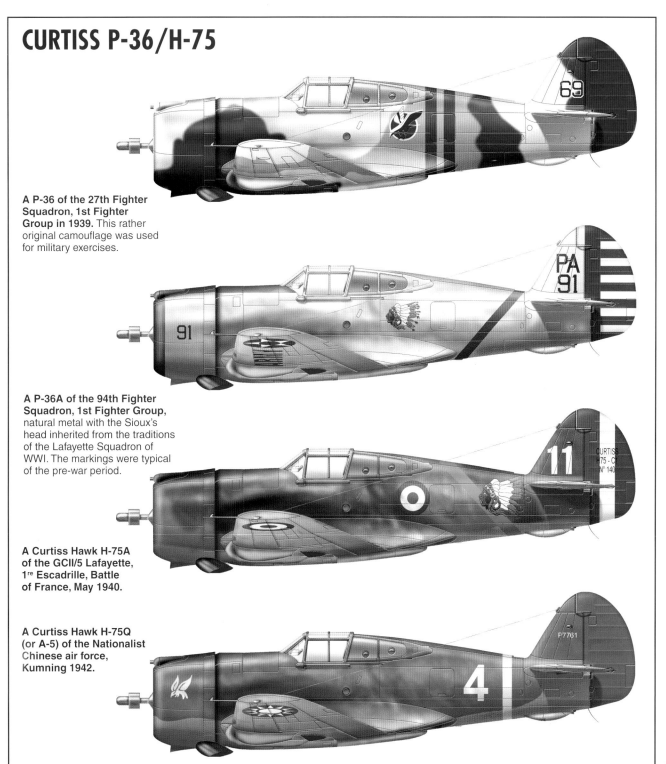

A P-36 of the 27th Fighter Squadron, 1st Fighter Group in 1939. This rather original camouflage was used for military exercises.

A P-36A of the 94th Fighter Squadron, 1st Fighter Group, natural metal with the Sioux's head inherited from the traditions of the Lafayette Squadron of WWI. The markings were typical of the pre-war period.

A Curtiss Hawk H-75A of the GCII/5 Lafayette, 1ʳᵉ Escadrille, Battle of France, May 1940.

A Curtiss Hawk H-75Q (or A-5) of the Nationalist Chinese air force, Kumning 1942.

The P-40 PROTOTYPES

As it was quite clear that the radial engine was going to be outclassed by what was being produced in the West and among the competition, in February 1937, the Air Corps asked for a fighter equipped with the new Allison V-1710 inline engine which had just been completed and to which a supercharger had to be added as the plane had been designed for low altitudes. This gave birth to the XP-37, based on an H-75B airframe and keeping its wings, landing gear and part of the tail. The front part of the plane was however much more aerodynamic in order to accommodate the new powerplant. With new ethyl glycol and fuel tanks fitted between the cockpit and the nose - thereby pushing the cockpit further back - the aircraft resembled the famous racers of the period. Tested in July 1937, the XP-37 (serial n° 37-375) reached a speed of 342 mph thanks to the power output of 1150bhp from the new Allison engine, the V-1710-21. There was a noticeable drop in power at high altitude, visibility left a lot to be desired and vibrations appeared when the aircraft positioned itself for landing; nevertheless 13 examples were ordered in December 1937, the first one being delivered in April 1939 only because of the very slow production of the Allison engines.

Meanwhile, and especially because of the capricious behaviour of the turbochargers, an Allison V-1710-19 had been fitted to the tenth example of the P-36A (serial n° 38-010) to respect to a contract dated April 1938.

In this new configuration, the new machine was first designated H-75P, then XP-40 and first flew in October 1938. Compared with the XP-37 whose radiators were fitted between the engine and the cockpit, disappearing within the overall outline of the plane, the cooling system on this new model was placed under the fuselage, and the silhouette was not unlike that of the P-36 since the cockpit was moved back to its original central position over the wings.

The performance did not live up to expectations with a maximum speed of only 300 mph and a cruising speed of 202 mph. All un-aerodynamic features on the fuselage were eliminated, the exhaust pipes were modified, the radiator was placed under the nose, the air-intake on the engine cowling was removed, others were installed in the wing roots for the oil radiators, and the wing leading edges were given a slight angle. Finally, on 25 January 1939, the prototype H-75P reached 343.75 mph during a new competition organised at Wright Field, 15 mph less than the firm was counting on.

At this stage of the project, only the restricted speed of the H-75P prevented Curtiss from being awarded a big contract with the US Army Air Corps. Work was taken up again frantically, trying to remove anything un-

The XP-40 in its original configuration, recognisable by its radiator which was placed further back. The nose here still covered with all sorts of things sticking out was streamlined out for the second model. The plane was however very close to the first production P-40s, except for the lower intake and the undercarriage doors. *(DR)*

aerodynamic (replacing round-headed rivets with flush ones, on the canopy slides, reworking the shape of the engine cowling, installing a new air intake system, installing individual pipes to increase thrust, redesigning the wings, returning to straight leading edges).

This persistence was rewarded by a contract dated 24 April 1939 for 524 H-81A worth $12 872 898, which was a record for a US-made plane.

The prototype's radiator intake size and the machine gun streamlining were further modified and the model was finally completed at the end of the year. After a first test flight in the hands of L. Child, the Curtiss chief test pilot on 4 April 1940, production began in May of the same year.

Very manoeuvrable and fast with its 360 mph, the new H-81A (P-40 CU the suffix designating Curtiss) had the advantage that it could also be mass-produced more cheaply than its main rivals at a time when the sound of marching boots was getting louder and louder in Europe and Asia.

The rare XP-37s which were built were given to evaluation units where some were camouflaged with experimental schemes. The air intakes on the sides were some of the characteristics together with the cockpit which was placed further back towards the tail.
(USAAF)

P-40 PROTOTYPES

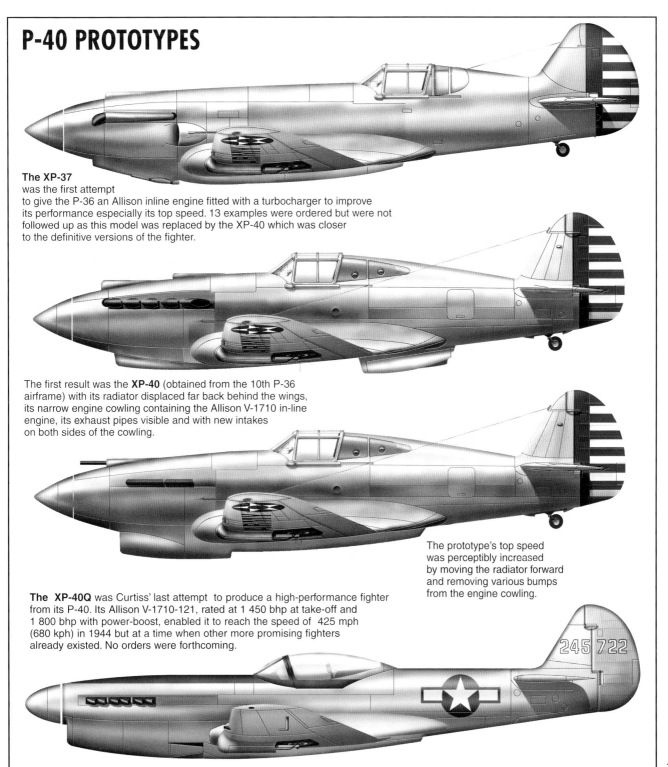

The XP-37
was the first attempt
to give the P-36 an Allison inline engine fitted with a turbocharger to improve
its performance especially its top speed. 13 examples were ordered but were not
followed up as this model was replaced by the XP-40 which was closer
to the definitive versions of the fighter.

The first result was the **XP-40** (obtained from the 10th P-36
airframe) with its radiator displaced far back behind the wings,
its narrow engine cowling containing the Allison V-1710 in-line
engine, its exhaust pipes visible and with new intakes
on both sides of the cowling.

The prototype's top speed
was perceptibly increased
by moving the radiator forward
and removing various bumps
from the engine cowling.

The XP-40Q was Curtiss' last attempt to produce a high-performance fighter
from its P-40. Its Allison V-1710-121, rated at 1 450 bhp at take-off and
1 800 bhp with power-boost, enabled it to reach the speed of 425 mph
(680 kph) in 1944 but at a time when other more promising fighters
already existed. No orders were forthcoming.

The CURTISS P-40CU and P-40B/C

Technically the aircraft was a monocoque monoplane, all-metal except for the fabric-covered metal structure of the wing and tail moving surfaces. The wings had a NACA 2215 profile tending towards a NACA 2209 at the wing tips which had already been tried out on the P-36.

The fuel which was stored in four wing tanks between the fillet radius and the landing gear and a fifth behind the pilot (988 litres in all) supplied a1040 bhp Allison V-1710-33 engine. Armament was rather feeble for the times as far as Western counterparts were concerned and consisted of two Colt-Browning 12,7 mm machine guns housed in the engine cowling. The landing gear was entirely retractable but left a part of the tyres visible; the tailwheel was completely hidden. Note that the prototype had two trap doors on the undercarriage legs near the torsion links and two front trap doors at the root of the struts; these disappeared with the model under discussion here.

Production was kept up well since by September 1940, 168 P-40 had been delivered. It was the 8th Pursuit Group made up of the 33rd, 35th and 36th Pursuit Squadrons at Langley Field in Virginia which got them first, then the 20th Pursuit Group (55th, 77th, 79th Pursuit Squadrons) based at March Field in California, then the 31st Pursuit Group (39th, 40th, 41st Pursuit Squadrons) based at Selfridge, Michigan and then, very briefly, the 35th Pursuit Group (21st, 34th, 70th Pursuit Squadrons).

Meanwhile in March 1940, it was decided to honour a large order dating back to October 1939 for 230 Curtiss H-81As (the export designation for the first P-40s) ordered by France. These machines could be fitted with four Browning FN 38 7.5 mm machine guns in the wings and be equipped with French equipment.

They never reached their destination, and thanks to the British Purchasing Commission, in September 1940, a first batch of 140 machines (serial N° AH-741 to 880) was acquired by the RAF, which immediately drew attention to certain deficiencies like the absence of cockpit armour, the lack of self-sealing tanks, the weak armament despite the installation of the four wing-mounted Browning 7.7 mm machine guns. The official British designation changed from Tomahawk MkI/MkIA to MkIB.

These planes were delivered to a large number of squadrons (2, 13, 16, 26, 94, 112, 168, 171, 208, 231, 241, 250, 260, 349, 414, 430 and 613) but never really had the favour of the authorities who relegated them to training and to ground support in North Africa mainly with the Desert Air Force. The remainder of the French order, 90 planes, was also taken up by the RAF (together with another batch of 20 machines, serial numbers AH881-990) who obviously insisted on the fitting of more powerful armament, i.e. the four wing-mounted guns as well as those already fitted over the engine, and the protection for the pilot and the fuel tanks already mentioned. Indeed, the deficiencies already listed by the RAF had led Curtiss to bring out a new model, the H-81B, incorporating all the modifications mentioned as well as more powerful armament with 380 rounds instead of the original 200. This version was called the P-40B or Hawk 81A-2 (Tomahawk MkIIA) and delivered to the USAAC which had asked for 131 examples (serial N° 5205 to 5304 and 41-13297 to 13327) during the winter of 1940 and the spring of 1941.

The next stage was an order for 930 Hawk 81A-3s (Tomahawk MkIIBs) from Great Britain in which the radio equipment (SCR-274) and the fuel supply were modified; armament was still four Browning 7.7 mm machine guns in the wings as well as the two 12.7 mm

British Tomahawk Mk I 26 Squadron based at Gatwick taxiing. The ground crewman is putting all his weight on the tail to stop the tail wheel from vibrating and wobbling. Some of the planes in this squadron had cameras installed on the roundels on the left side of the fuselage. *(DR)*

guns over the engine. A lot of machines (about 300) were then transferred to other allies like China and Russia which greatly needed high performance fighters.

The interest which the British order aroused prompted Curtiss to develop the H-81B, or the P-40C which took into account all the previous modifications (self-sealing tanks, wing- and engine-mounted guns with 490 rounds, new SCR-274 radio) as well as provision for a 197 litre drop tank. The USAAC ordered 193 examples, and production started in the spring of 1941. Deliveries first went to the 36th Pursuit Group in Puerto Rico and the 16th Pursuit Group (24th, 29th, 43rd Pursuit Squadrons) based at Panama; after that, other units already equipped with the P-40B, like the 8th and the 18th Pursuit Groups, were given them.

The first P-40s saw service on many fronts particularly Russia which received 146 Tomahawk IIBs taken from British stocks together with 49 others coming directly from factories in the USA. They were used in the defence of Leningrad and Moscow during the winter of 1941-42. Other small batches from England were sent to Egypt and Turkey.

Apart from the North African operations, the RAF used them over the Channel with Nos 2, 26, 231and 241 Squadrons, in the Middle East against Vichy, and two others, Nos 400 and 403 operated in the Royal Canadian Air Force.

When the Japanese attacked Pearl Harbor on 7 December 1941, the 15th and 18th Pursuit Groups at Wheeler Field lost 62 P-40Bs on the ground and the 4th Pursuit Group based a Bellows Field lost 10 P-40Cs out of 12.

This chapter cannot be closed without mentioning the historic epic of the Flying Tigers. Set up by a forceful character, General Claire Lee Chennault, with the tacit approval of the American author-

A nice line up of Curtiss P-40B Tomahawks, ready for a mission with 250 Squadron. *(Royal Australian Air Force)*

This P-40 from the beginning of the series constitutes rather a mystery as much by its camouflage -which may mean it was being transferred to a friendly country (France?) - as by the white stripe painted across the middle of the tail fin. (DR)

ities in order to contain the Japanese advance in China and Burma, and relieve Tchang Kai Tchek's nationalist troops, this air force was equipped with about a hundred British Tomahawk MkIIs worth $8.9 m by the Chinese, flown by American volunteers, some of doubtful reputation, for 600 to 750 dollars a month, which was a real godsend even without the 500 dollars paid in gold for every Japanese plane brought down in aerial combat.

In six months' operations, the three squadrons «Adam and Eve», «Panda Bear» and «Hell's Angels» destroyed 286 planes in the air and 240 on the ground for the loss of only 16 planes (four in the air, six during ground attacks, three through accidents and three during air raids).

In July 1942, the AVG (American Volunteer group) was incorporated into the 23rd Fighter group and carried on the war against the Japanese, but this time officially. It was the beginning of the Curtiss fighter's legend.

P-40C Technical Specifications

Power Plant:
One Allison V-171-33 rated at 1040 bhp at take-off and 1090 bhp at 4 metres (13 123 ft), fitted with a Curtiss Electric constant speed 3.36 metre (11 feet) propeller.

Dimensions
Wingspan: 11.38 metres (37 ft 4 in)
Length: 9.68 metres (31 ft 9 in)
Wing area: 22 sq. metres (236 sq. ft)
Height: 3.23 metres (10 ft 7 in)
Weight Empty: 2636kg (5600 lbs)
Loaded: 3393 kg (7464 lbs)

Performance
Max. Speed: between 550 and 565 kph (344 mph and 353 mph) at 4 500 m; 450kph (281 mph) at 9 000m
Cruising speed: 435 kph (272 mph)
Rate of Climb: 810 m (2 656 ft)/ min.
Ceiling: 8,850m (29 028 ft) to 9,000m (29 520 ft)
Range: 1,168km (730 miles) and 1 968 km (1 230miles) with drop tank
Armament:
Six machine guns (two 12.7 mm Browning M-2s over the engine and four Colt-Browning 7.7 mm MG-40s in the wings).

CURTISS P-40CU

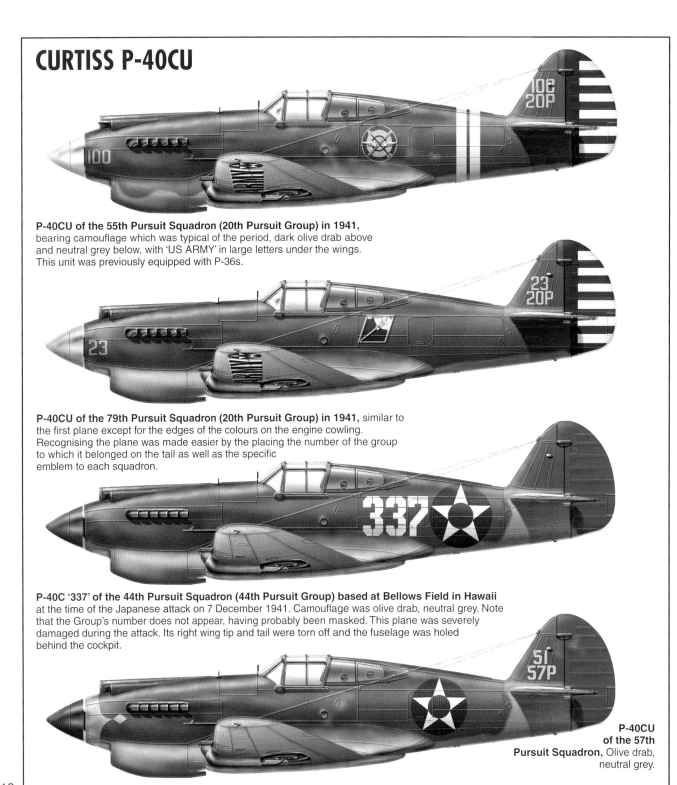

P-40CU of the 55th Pursuit Squadron (20th Pursuit Group) in 1941,
bearing camouflage which was typical of the period, dark olive drab above
and neutral grey below, with 'US ARMY' in large letters under the wings.
This unit was previously equipped with P-36s.

P-40CU of the 79th Pursuit Squadron (20th Pursuit Group) in 1941, similar to
the first plane except for the edges of the colours on the engine cowling.
Recognising the plane was made easier by the placing the number of the group
to which it belonged on the tail as well as the specific
emblem to each squadron.

P-40C '337' of the 44th Pursuit Squadron (44th Pursuit Group) based at Bellows Field in Hawaii
at the time of the Japanese attack on 7 December 1941. Camouflage was olive drab, neutral grey. Note
that the Group's number does not appear, having probably been masked. This plane was severely
damaged during the attack. Its right wing tip and tail were torn off and the fuselage was holed
behind the cockpit.

**P-40CU
of the 57th
Pursuit Squadron,** Olive drab,
neutral grey.

18

CURTISS P-40B/C

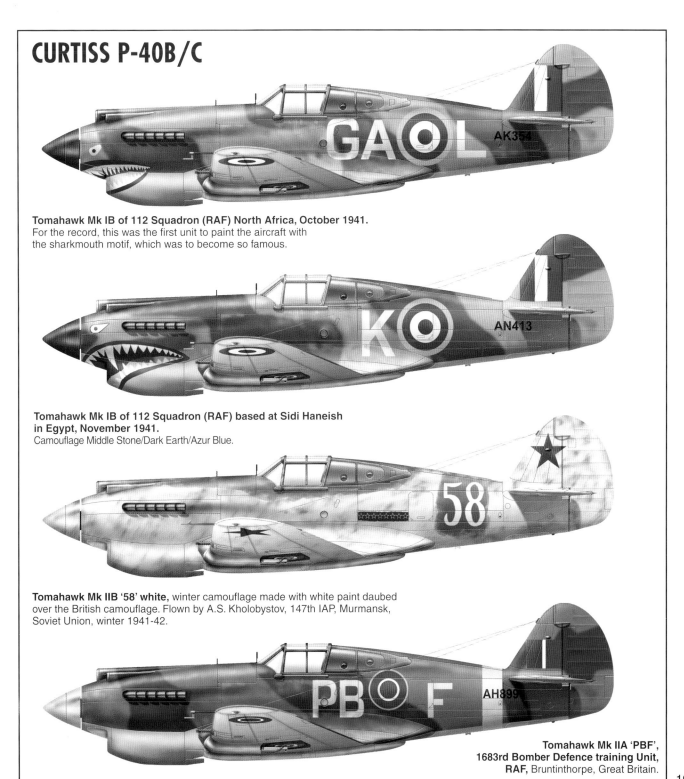

Tomahawk Mk IB of 112 Squadron (RAF) North Africa, October 1941.
For the record, this was the first unit to paint the aircraft with
the sharkmouth motif, which was to become so famous.

**Tomahawk Mk IB of 112 Squadron (RAF) based at Sidi Haneish
in Egypt, November 1941.**
Camouflage Middle Stone/Dark Earth/Azur Blue.

Tomahawk Mk IIB '58' white, winter camouflage made with white paint daubed
over the British camouflage. Flown by A.S. Kholobystov, 147th IAP, Murmansk,
Soviet Union, winter 1941-42.

**Tomahawk Mk IIA 'PBF',
1683rd Bomber Defence training Unit,
RAF,** Bruntinthorpe, Great Britain.

19

CURTISS P-40CU, P-40B/C

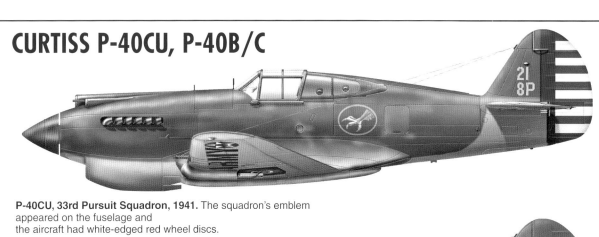

P-40CU, 33rd Pursuit Squadron, 1941. The squadron's emblem
appeared on the fuselage and
the aircraft had white-edged red wheel discs.

P-40CU, 35th Pursuit Squadron, end 1941. At the time the nationality roundels
had replaced the unit insignia on the fuselage. The red, white and blue nationality
markings on the tail have been painted over with olive drab;
the white band indicates a unit commander.

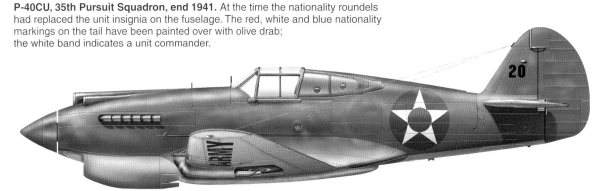

**P-40B, 33rd Pursuit Squadron (8th Fighter Group), based at Rekjavik
in Iceland, September 1941.** Olive drab and neutral grey camouflage.

**P-40C, 33rd Fighter Squadron
(8th Fighter Group),** Iceland, August 1941.

CURTISS P-40B/HAWK 81A-2

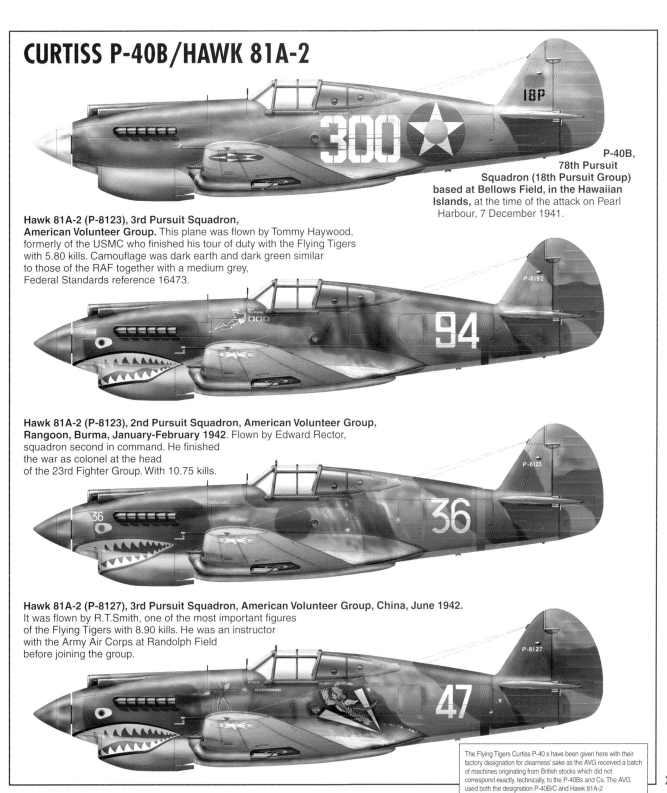

P-40B, 78th Pursuit Squadron (18th Pursuit Group) based at Bellows Field, in the Hawaiian Islands, at the time of the attack on Pearl Harbour, 7 December 1941.

Hawk 81A-2 (P-8123), 3rd Pursuit Squadron, American Volunteer Group. This plane was flown by Tommy Haywood, formerly of the USMC who finished his tour of duty with the Flying Tigers with 5.80 kills. Camouflage was dark earth and dark green similar to those of the RAF together with a medium grey, Federal Standards reference 16473.

Hawk 81A-2 (P-8123), 2nd Pursuit Squadron, American Volunteer Group, Rangoon, Burma, January-February 1942. Flown by Edward Rector, squadron second in command. He finished the war as colonel at the head of the 23rd Fighter Group. With 10.75 kills.

Hawk 81A-2 (P-8127), 3rd Pursuit Squadron, American Volunteer Group, China, June 1942. It was flown by R.T.Smith, one of the most important figures of the Flying Tigers with 8.90 kills. He was an instructor with the Army Air Corps at Randolph Field before joining the group.

The Flying Tigers Curtiss P-40 s have been given here with their factory designation for clearness' sake as the AVG received a batch of machines originating from British stocks which did not correspond exactly, technically, to the P-40Bs and Cs. The AVG used both the designation P-40B/C and Hawk 81A-2

HAWK 81A-2

**Hawk 81A-2 (P-8156), 74th Fighter Squadron (23rd Fighter Group),
Kunling, China September 1942.** At the time, the AVG had gone back
to the ranks of the US Air Force

**Hawk H81-A2 (P-8134), 2nd Pursuit Squadron
(American Volunteer Group) China 1941.**
Flown by David Lee 'Tex' Hill, 11.25 kills
with the Flying Tigers

**Hawk 81A-2 (P-8178 sometimes given as P-8198), 1st Pursuit Squadron
(American Volunteer Group) Loiwing China April 1942,** flown by
the second in command of the squadron,
Charles R. Bond, 8 kills with the Flying Tigers.

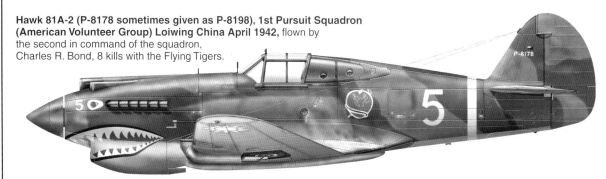

Hawk 81A-2 (P-8194), 1st Pursuit Squadron, Kunming, China, June 1942.
Flown by First Squadron Leader Robert Neale, 15.55 kills with
the Flying Tigers and the top American ace
at the time the group was disbanded.

TOMAHAWK Mk. I/Mk. II

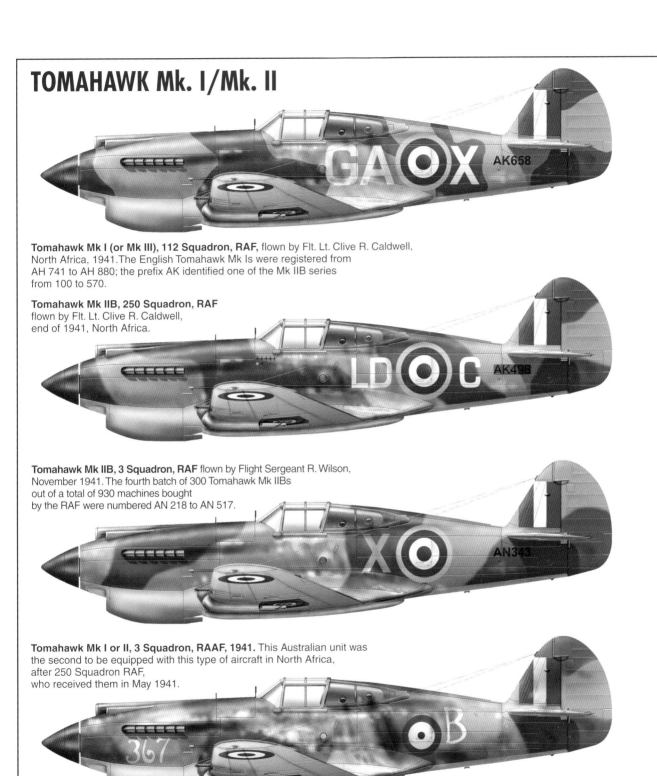

Tomahawk Mk I (or Mk III), 112 Squadron, RAF, flown by Flt. Lt. Clive R. Caldwell, North Africa, 1941. The English Tomahawk Mk Is were registered from AH 741 to AH 880; the prefix AK identified one of the Mk IIB series from 100 to 570.

Tomahawk Mk IIB, 250 Squadron, RAF flown by Flt. Lt. Clive R. Caldwell, end of 1941, North Africa.

Tomahawk Mk IIB, 3 Squadron, RAF flown by Flight Sergeant R. Wilson, November 1941. The fourth batch of 300 Tomahawk Mk IIBs out of a total of 930 machines bought by the RAF were numbered AN 218 to AN 517.

Tomahawk Mk I or II, 3 Squadron, RAAF, 1941. This Australian unit was the second to be equipped with this type of aircraft in North Africa, after 250 Squadron RAF, who received them in May 1941.

The CURTISS P-40 D/E

As was often the case the engineers at Curtiss were already studying the next model, the P-40D of which however only a small number were brought out, about forty. The new version's first flight took place on 22 May 1940, scarcely a month and eighteen days after the firstP-40.

It was a question of engines. Whereas the V-1170-33 which equipped the P-40CU (the official designation of the models based on the second prototype of the XP-40), i.e.the P-40B and C, could only produce 1090bhp with power boosting, the new V-1170-39-F3R which gave 1150bhp up to a height of 3 560 m (11 640 ft) for about thirty minutes, increasing to 1 470 bhp for five minutes which was a significant gain in time of war. Its installation meant that there were some important changes. The upper air intake was lengthened, its round cross-section became oval, the engine cowling was redesigned, the propeller boss fitted the nose more closely. The instrument panel was modified because the machine guns had been removed; a new canopy was installed with two supports on the windshield and the rear glass panels increased in size for better visibility; the fuselage was slightly shortened, the cockpit was lowered slightly as a result of the removal of the cowling-mounted machine guns; the undercarriage was shorter with new kinematics; pilot protection was also improved and a central pylon for a 197 litre drop tank or a 227kg bomb was installed. Apart from hydraulic feeding for the guns, the new model had 12.7 mm guns with 615 rounds each, 20 mm cannon replacing these if desired. All these changes made the British, who were always careful to give their planes national names, christen this plane the Kittyhawk Mk I whereas Curtiss had given it the name Hawk 87A-1. Only 22 P-40D were delivered to the US Army Air Corps (serial numbers 40 359, 40-361 to 40-381) and to the British (AK 571 to AK 591) out of an order for 560 machines, dating from May 1940. The order was changed to one for an improved version the Hawk 87A-2, or the P-40E or Kittyhawk Mk 1A, armed with six wing-mounted machine guns in response to a request from the USAAC.

This was the first model of the P-40 to be produced in large numbers, with 820 being ordered by the USAAC in February 1941 and which were delivered from

29 August of the same year until May 1942; the order was followed by another for 1 500 machines, P-40 E - 1s this time with

pylons for three bombs under the wings, for the USAAF (United States Army Air Force) - the USAAC having changed its name since June 1941. The performance of the new model, now unofficially called the Warhawk, was a major leap forward with its top speed of 356 mph, its still impressive dive, its improve protection and its pylons which improved its tactical capacity despite a certain directional instability at low speeds which caused problems at landing and take-off. All the 2320 machines which were produced (more than any other version except for the P-40N) were sent to the USAAF (820 machines, serial numbers 40-358, 40-382 to 40-681, 41-5305 to 41-5744 and 41-13521 to 41-13599), the RAF which received 540 P-40 E-1s out of an initial order for 560 (serial numbers 41-24766 to 41-25195, 41-35874 to 41-36953) and Allied countries (Canada, Australia, South Africa, USSR, etc) who received 960 P-40 E-1s. Thirty went to the AVG. It is to be noted that some P-40 E-1s from the end of the series had a dorsal fin fitted which became standard in order to reduce swing on take-off. It was also converted into a two-seater for training purposes; this was not a great success. It was also equipped to carry 227 kg bombs, this not being successful either.

The Warhawk was the first version to be engaged in large numbers by the new USAAF (although some had been present at Pearl Harbor) which sent some squadrons to China where they reinforced the strength of Claire Lee Chennault's 10th Air Force (which was replaced by the 14th Air Force in March 1943) after absorbing the Flying Tigers into the 23rd Fighter Group and changing the three initial Pursuit Squadrons (1st, 2nd and 3rd) into the 74th, 75th and 76th Fighter Squadrons. They took part also in the defence of the Aleutian Islands, which was a thankless task, together with the 11th Fighter Squadron of the 343rd Fighter Group - whose machines were recognisable by the yellow and black Tiger's head and the white stripes on the fuselage and the tail - and operated with a Canadian unit, 14 Squadron, RCAF, from April 1942.

At the beginning of 1942, as the air raid launched on 19 February against Darwin (when 8 out of ten P-40s were lost) demonstrated, the Japanese thrust had to be contained if Australian towns and industrial centres were to be spared. The 7th, 8th and 9th Fighter Squadrons of the famous 49th Fighter Group were hurried to Bankston, Fairbairn and Williamtown in the middle of March under RAAF command.

This was news as the 49th Fighter Group was the first unit to be entirely deployed in the war zone since Pearl Harbour. The situation improved fairly quickly, especially after the Japanese defeat in the Battle of the Coral Sea at the beginning of May which took Japanese pressure off Port Moresby in Papua New Guinea. It was at this time that more effective tactics were perfected for fighting against the agile Zero (which were very similar to those put into practice by Chennault with the Flying Tigers in China) by exploit-

These ground crew are checking this Kittyhawk Mk Ia (P-40E)'s wing-mounted machine guns and cleaning their breaches, 111 Squadron, RCAF at Kodiak, Alaska, June 1941. This unit took part, with others (14, 115, and 118 Squadrons RCAF and the USAAF 343rd Fighter Group) in the defence of the northern sector of the American continent against the Japanese. (DR)

ing to their utmost the qualities of the P-40 whose diving was exactly what was required for surprise attacks with the advantage of height. It could thus dive, maintain its speed, gain height again and the dive again on another target: the classic 'hit and run' which was so dear to the Americans and so effective, especially against opponents whose strength lay in the roll.

The British Kittyhawk 1s were mainly engaged in North Africa and in the Middle East as fighter-bombers where they showed again how robust they were and how good they were at ground attack.

Specifications for the P-40E

Powerplant
One Allison V-1710-39 rated at 1 150 bhp

Dimensions
Wingspan: 37 ft 4 ins (11.38 m)
Length: 30 ft 9 ins (9.50 m) Sources consulted do not agree on this point. Some give 31 ft 6 ins (9.68 m) whereas the fuselage was reduced by 6 inches (15 cm) on the engine cowling compared with the P-40B/C.
Wing surface: 2136 sq. ft.
Height: 12 ft 4 ins (3.76 m)

Weight
Unloaded: 6 336 lbs (2 880 kg)

Loaded: 8 270 lbs (3 759 kg)
Max. All-up weight: 9190 lbs (4 177 kg)

Performance
Max. Speed: 367 mph (588 kph) at 14 868 ft (4 575 m)
Cruising Speed: 309 mph (495 kph)
Climb Rate: 2 031 ft/ min (625 m/ min)
Ceiling: 28 762 ft (8 850 m)
Range: 703 miles (1 126 km) in combat, maximum 955 miles (1 529 km)

Armament
Six Colt- Browning 12.7 mm M-2 machine guns.

CURTISS P-40E

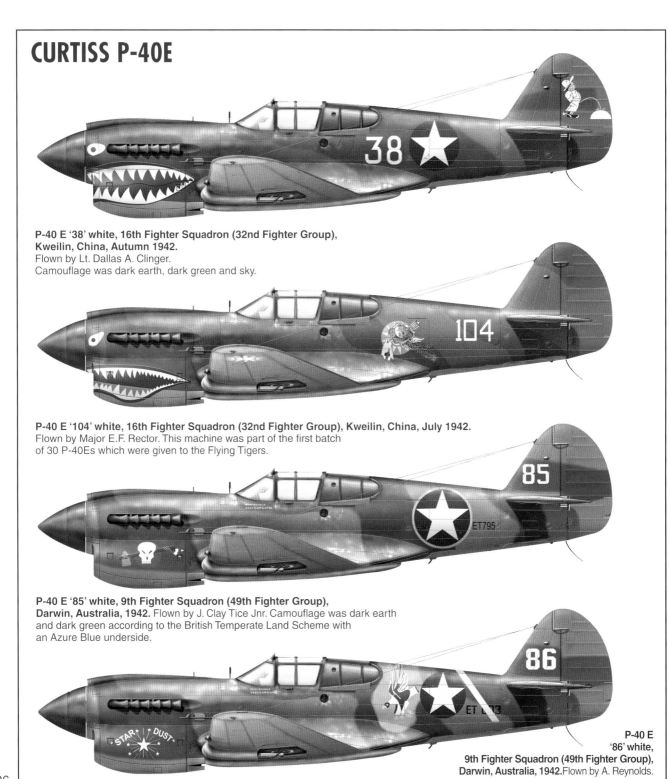

P-40 E '38' white, 16th Fighter Squadron (32nd Fighter Group),
Kweilin, China, Autumn 1942.
Flown by Lt. Dallas A. Clinger.
Camouflage was dark earth, dark green and sky.

P-40 E '104' white, 16th Fighter Squadron (32nd Fighter Group), Kweilin, China, July 1942.
Flown by Major E.F. Rector. This machine was part of the first batch
of 30 P-40Es which were given to the Flying Tigers.

P-40 E '85' white, 9th Fighter Squadron (49th Fighter Group),
Darwin, Australia, 1942. Flown by J. Clay Tice Jnr. Camouflage was dark earth
and dark green according to the British Temperate Land Scheme with
an Azure Blue underside.

P-40 E
'86' white,
9th Fighter Squadron (49th Fighter Group),
Darwin, Australia, 1942. Flown by A. Reynolds.

CURTISS P-40E

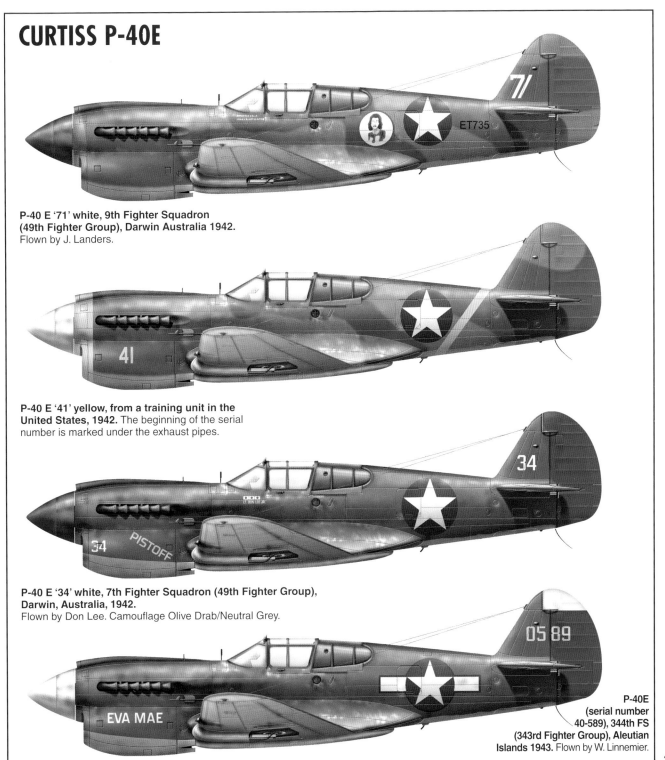

P-40 E '71' white, 9th Fighter Squadron
(49th Fighter Group), Darwin Australia 1942.
Flown by J. Landers.

P-40 E '41' yellow, from a training unit in the
United States, 1942. The beginning of the serial
number is marked under the exhaust pipes.

P-40 E '34' white, 7th Fighter Squadron (49th Fighter Group),
Darwin, Australia, 1942.
Flown by Don Lee. Camouflage Olive Drab/Neutral Grey.

P-40E
(serial number
40-589), 344th FS
(343rd Fighter Group), Aleutian
Islands 1943. Flown by W. Linnemier.

CURTISS P-40E

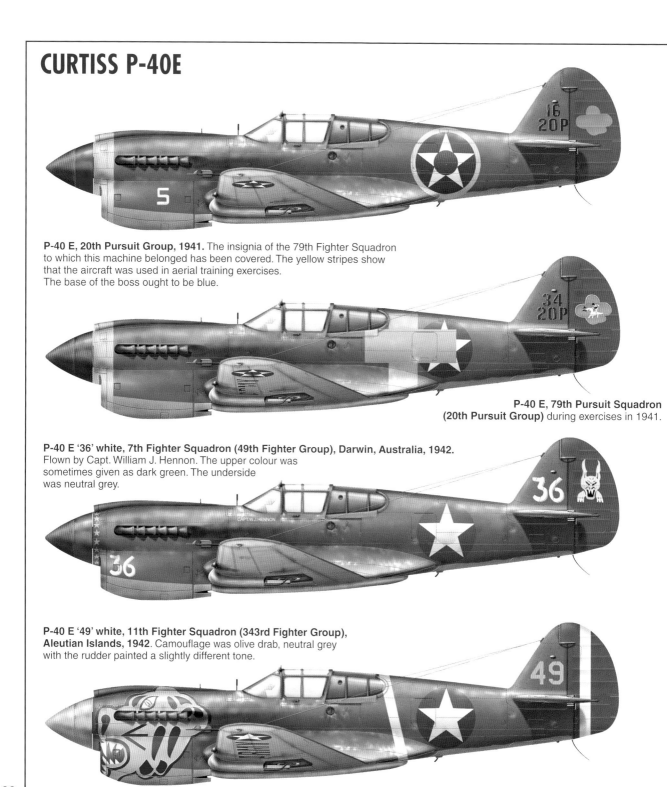

P-40 E, 20th Pursuit Group, 1941. The insignia of the 79th Fighter Squadron
to which this machine belonged has been covered. The yellow stripes show
that the aircraft was used in aerial training exercises.
The base of the boss ought to be blue.

**P-40 E, 79th Pursuit Squadron
(20th Pursuit Group)** during exercises in 1941.

P-40 E '36' white, 7th Fighter Squadron (49th Fighter Group), Darwin, Australia, 1942.
Flown by Capt. William J. Hennon. The upper colour was
sometimes given as dark green. The underside
was neutral grey.

**P-40 E '49' white, 11th Fighter Squadron (343rd Fighter Group),
Aleutian Islands, 1942.** Camouflage was olive drab, neutral grey
with the rudder painted a slightly different tone.

CURTISS P-40E

P-40 E 8th Fighter Squadron (49th Fighter Group,
Dobodura, New Guinea, April 1943.
Flown by Ellis Wright.

This brightly-coloured
machine had wavy red and yellow
wheel discs.

P-40 E 11th Fighter Squadron (343rd Fighter Group),
Adak, Alaska September 1942. The Aleutian Tiger's head has been touched
up with olive green to allow the insignia of the 11th Fighter Squadron to be applied.
The white stripes enabled the P-40s based
in the far north to be recognised.

P-40 E, 9th Fighter Squadron (49th Fighter Group),
Darwin, Australia, 1942. Flown by Lt. Bob Vaught. Note the rather
original shark's head on black background.

P-40 E, 11th Fighter Squadron (343rd Fighter Group), Aleutian Islands, 1943.
The colour shots of these machines painted in olive drab, show, more or less,
long medium green blotches, on the wing tips and the tail.

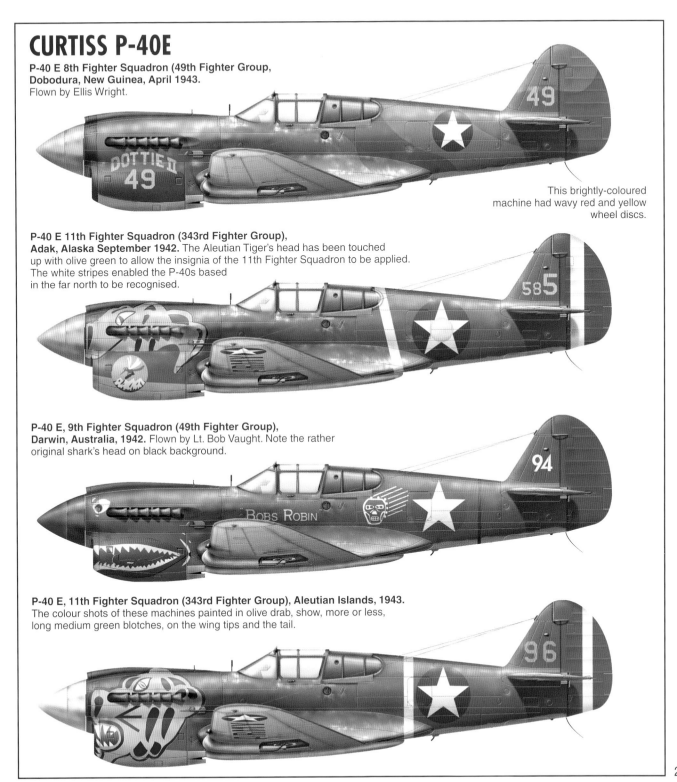

29

CURTISS P-40E

Camouflage.
upper surfaces dark earth FS 30 118, dark green FS
34 096. The underside shown here has probably been
painted light blue 27 (sky blue) since this plane, ET
601, came from RAF stocks. Other sources give a
medium green 42 (between FS 34 092 and FS 34
108), sand (FS 34 133) and azure blue underside
(FS 35 231), or medium green, sand and bright sky
blue.

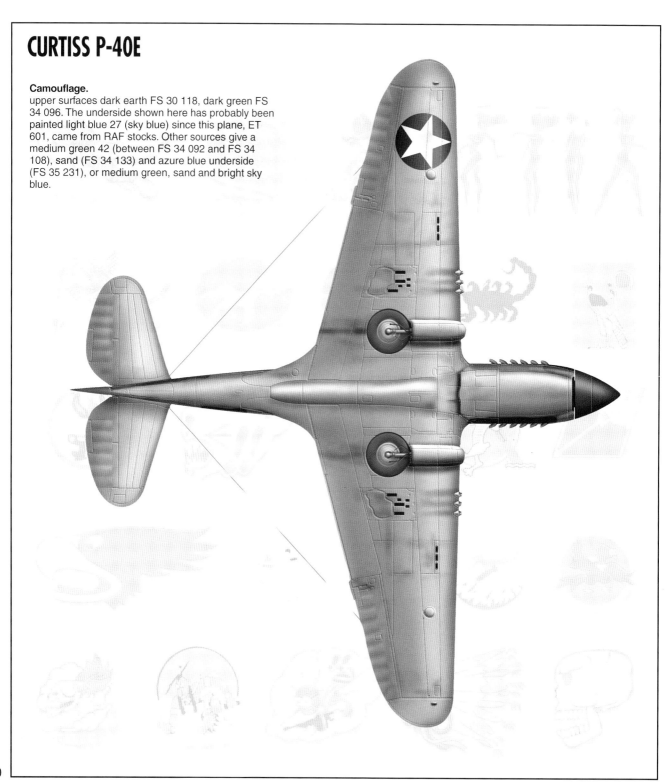

CURTISS P-40E

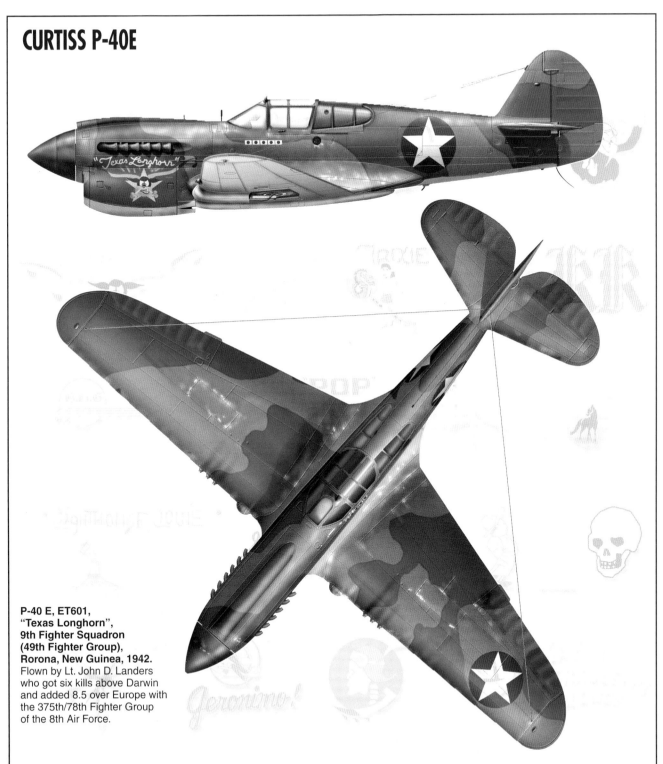

**P-40 E, ET601,
"Texas Longhorn",
9th Fighter Squadron
(49th Fighter Group),
Rorona, New Guinea, 1942.**
Flown by Lt. John D. Landers
who got six kills above Darwin
and added 8.5 over Europe with
the 375th/78th Fighter Group
of the 8th Air Force.

CURTISS P-40E

P-40 E, '15' yellow, 7th Fighter Squadron (49th Fighter Group),
Darwin, Australia, 1942. Flown by Lt. Edgar Ball.

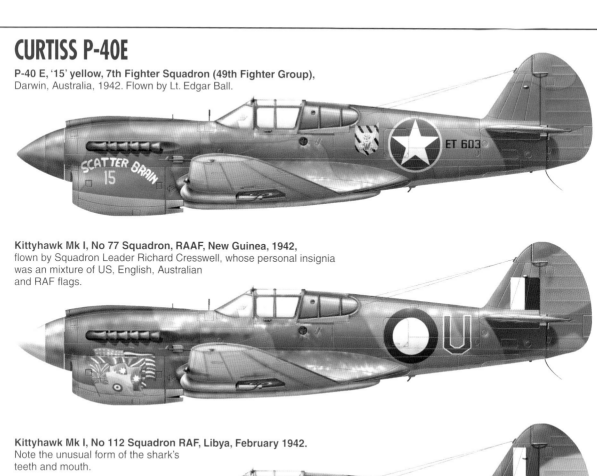

Kittyhawk Mk I, No 77 Squadron, RAAF, New Guinea, 1942,
flown by Squadron Leader Richard Cresswell, whose personal insignia
was an mixture of US, English, Australian
and RAF flags.

Kittyhawk Mk I, No 112 Squadron RAF, Libya, February 1942.
Note the unusual form of the shark's
teeth and mouth.

Kittyhawk Mk IA, No112 Squadron RAF, Egypt, October 1942.
Here the shark's teeth are more to type. Camouflage is standard
for the North African theatre: dark earth, middle stone
and azure blue as on the previous machine.

CURTISS P-40E

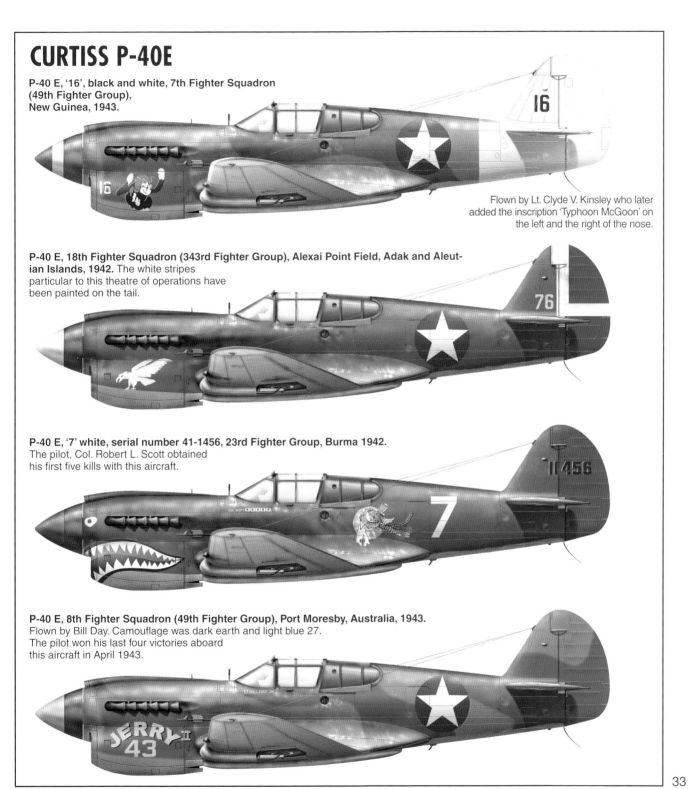

P-40 E, '16', black and white, 7th Fighter Squadron
(49th Fighter Group),
New Guinea, 1943.

Flown by Lt. Clyde V. Kinsley who later
added the inscription 'Typhoon McGoon' on
the left and the right of the nose.

P-40 E, 18th Fighter Squadron (343rd Fighter Group), Alexai Point Field, Adak and Aleutian Islands, 1942. The white stripes
particular to this theatre of operations have
been painted on the tail.

P-40 E, '7' white, serial number 41-1456, 23rd Fighter Group, Burma 1942.
The pilot, Col. Robert L. Scott obtained
his first five kills with this aircraft.

P-40 E, 8th Fighter Squadron (49th Fighter Group), Port Moresby, Australia, 1943.
Flown by Bill Day. Camouflage was dark earth and light blue 27.
The pilot won his last four victories aboard
this aircraft in April 1943.

33

The CURTISS P-40F

This version was the first serious attempt by the Curtiss design team to solve the problems which had been noted previously: directional instability at slow speeds particularly on take off, limited low engine speed at altitude limiting the plane to the ground attack role since its reputation in a dog-fight * was not brilliant. The solution came from England, which was producing the Rolls Royce Merlin 28, a two-stage engine fitted with a turbocharger which generated the required extra speed which the Allison V-1170-39 cruelly lacked above 15 000 feet (4,575m). Planned at the end of 1940, this engine change was carried out on a P-40D airframe (serial No 40-360) at the beginning of 1941 and the prototype designated XP-40F made its maiden flight in June of the same year. The trials showed that apart from the engine fitting the airframe well, the aircraft's quality had not suffered and that the prototype was almost as fast at 20 000 feet as the P-40 E at 15 000. It was decided to mass-produce the new machine and two contracts were signed, one for the production under licence of the English engine which became the Packard Merlin V-15600-1, and the other for 1 311 examples of the P-40F (Hawk 87B in its factory designation and Kittyhawk for the English).

In terms of power, the new Packard V-1560 produced 1 300 bhp at take-off, 1 240bhp at 11 375 feet and 1 120bhp at 18 330 ft, being also quieter and more regular than the Merlin. The shape of the plane was thus modified and the long carburettor air-intake over the engine cowling was repositioned inside the large lower intake which itself became deeper as it now held different kinds of radiators. The fuel tank was increased by 30 litres, the main wing tanks being set out differently; the P-40F was equipped with central underbelly pylons to take drop tanks or 227 kg or 405 kg bombs.

The first 699 P-4F built and delivered between January and August 1942 (96 P-400F-CUs, serial numbers 41-13660 to 41-13965 and 603 P-40F-1-CUs, serial numbers 41-13967 to 41-14229) still had directional sta-

On this P-40F-5, 33rd Fighter Group, it can be clearly seen that the tail has been moved further back. This change refined the silhouette of the plane and was introduced to improve stability. 'Dammit' was launched from the aircraft carrier USS Ranger, during Operation 'Torch', the landings in French North Africa in November 1942. (USAAF)

bility problems which had to be solved. The first attempts to rectify this consisted in a dorsal fin mounted on some P-40F-1s linking the base of the tail fin to the middle of the fuselage, but the results were not convincing. Starting from the following lots of 123 P-40F-5CUs (serial numbers 41-14423 to 41-14599, delivered in August 1942), 177 P-40F-10CUs (serial numbers 41-14423 to 41-14599, delivered from October to November 1942), 200 P-40F-15 CUs (serial numbers 41-19733 to 41-19932, delivered in December 1942) and 112 P-40F-20CUs (serial numbers 41-19933 to 41-20044 delivered in January 1943), the fuselage was radically rethought and the tail fin was moved 18 inches (50.8 cms) further back along the fuselage, the horizontal tail surfaces remaining where they were. To this successful modification were added electrically operated radiator flaps from the P-40F-10 onwards, equipment for operating in cold climates especially for the machines sent to Alaska, and a controllable oxygen flow to replace the preceding constant flow system. Finally certain P-40F did not receive the new Packard V-1650-1 as it was not always easily available; they were equipped with the old Allison engine, becoming thus P-40R-1CUs and given over to training.

The Commonwealth (RAF, RAAF, SAAF) should have taken delivery of 330 P-40Fs, of which 230 were earmarked for the RAF only (serial numbers FL209 to FL 368 and FL 369 to FL 448) but it would appear that only 117 machines were received by these three forces; the rest en route to other allied forces, among whom the USSR which received a hun-

Specifications for the P-40F

Powerplant
One Packard V-1650 (Rolls Royce Merlin 28 built under licence) rated at 1 300bhp

Dimensions
Wingspan: 37 ft 4 ins (11.38 m)
Length: Standard fuselage: 31 ft 4 ins (9.65 m), **lengthened fuselage:** 33 ft (10.16 m)
Wing surface: 2136 sq. ft.
Height: 12 ft 4 ins (3.76 m)

Weight
Unloaded: 6 470 lbs (2 941 kg)
Loaded: 8 069 lbs (3 668 kg)
Max. All-up weight: 8 615 lbs (3 916 kg)

Performance
Max. Speed: 365 mph (585 kph) at 19 800 ft (6 096 m), 321 mph (515 kph) at 48 750 ft (1 500 m)
Cruising Speed: 302 mph (482 kph)
Climb Rate: 3 220 ft/min (991 m/min)
Ceiling: 33 990 ft (10 458 m)
Range: 605 miles (965 km), 1 508 miles (2 414 km) with drop tank.

Armament
Six 12.7 mm machine guns, 500 lb (227 kg) or 1 000lb (454 kg) bombs on under belly pylon, 100 lb (45 kg) bomb underwing

dred or so, and to the FAFL, (Forces Aériennes de la France Libre/Free French Air Force were either sunk during convoying or given back to the Americans (81 machines). It is worth noting that the British name of Kittyhawk for both the P-40F and P-40L does not make the task of identifying them any easier.

-The P-40F went into operational service during the summer of 1942 after the first deliveries to the USAAF in January of that year. It was the 57th Fighter Group (64th, 65th and 66th Fighter Squadrons) equipped with 75 P-40Fs from Mitchell Field in the States which was ready for action in North Africa from 1 September 1942, supporting the British

A P-40F-1 (serial number 41-14 295), 87th Fighter Squadron (79th Fighter Group, 9th Air Force), El Kabrit, in Egypt in January 1943. The X allowed aircraft from the 79th Fighter Group to be recognised. It was part of the first two batches of 699 P-40Fs built with a E's fuselage, i.e. without the lengthened tail. *(USAAF)*

forces who had been fighting the Italians, then the Germans, since 1940. The first kills were obtained on 9 August 1942, with two Me 109s shot down. The number of P-40Fs sent to the Mediterranean theatre increased with the preparations for Operation Torch, the invasion of North Africa under control of Vichy France, which began in November 1942. The 57th Fighter Group was then rejoined by the 33rd Fighter Group (58the, 59th and 60th Fighter Squadrons) and the 79th Fighter Group (85th, 86th and 87th Fighter Squadrons which were based in Morocco and Egypt. The P-40F's most famous feat of arms in the Mediterranean area was also one of the bloodiest and is now known as the 'Palm Sunday Massacre' : 18 April 1943, just after sundown off Cape Bon, the 57th Fighter Group, reinforced by the 314th Fighter Squadron (324th Fighter Group) as well as 92 Squadron RAF, came across a formation of 60 Ju-52s flying at low altitude and escorted by 21 Me 109, Bf 110 and Macchi C.202 fighters coming from Sicily. In the fight which followed, 46 P-40Fs covered by 11 Spitfires, fell upon on the unfortunate formation, shooting down no less than 59 Ju-52s and 16 fighters for the loss of only 6 of their own. The Germans only admitted losing 24Ju-52s, 35 others managing, according to their reports to reach the coast and carry out emergency landings.

The French received some P-40s for Commandant Rozannoff's GC II/5 on 8 January 1943 at Alger Maison-Blanche (see the article on this subject in *WING MASTERS* n° 11) which were kept until March 1943 when he received P-40Ls, lighter versions of the F. The P-40F was also used in the same theatre of operations by 260 Squadron RAF and 3 Squadron SAAF of the Western Desert Air Force until Italy's surrender in 1943.

---

* The expression 'Dog Fight' is used to describe aerial combat at close quarters where the fighters roll all around each other in order to get onto their opponent's tail for a good shot at him. This implies having a powerful enough engine and being very manoeuvrable in order to get out of the mélée if, and when, necessary.

CURTISS P-40F

**P-40F, serial number 41-14596, 64th Fighter Squadron
(57th Fighter Group), Scordia, Sicily 1943**
flown by Capt. Arthur E. Exon,
squadron commander.

Camouflage was dark earth,
middle stone, azure blue with
a touch of dark green around
the roundel.

**P-40F, '209' white, serial 41-13831, 68th Fighter Squadron (347th Fighter Group)
Guadalcanal, April 1943.** Camouflage was olive drab and neutral
grey with medium green blotches on the upper surfaces.
The white stripes denoted the theatre of operations.
Note the rather unusual form
of the shark's mouth.

P-40F, 318th Fighter Squadron (325th Fighter Group), North Africa, 1943
flown by Capt. Joseph A. Bloomer. The yellow and black checkerboard
on the tail was the mark of the 325th Fighter Group.

**P-40F, '44' white, 65th Fighter Squadron (57th Fighter Group),
North Africa, 1943.** Camouflage was sand 26 (FS 34133)
on neutral grey or azure blue underneath.

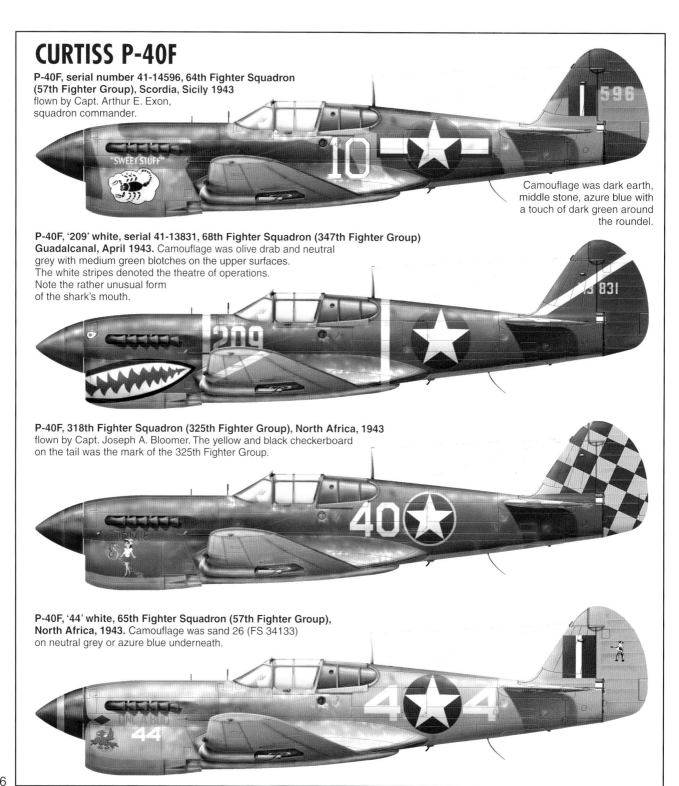

CURTISS P-40F

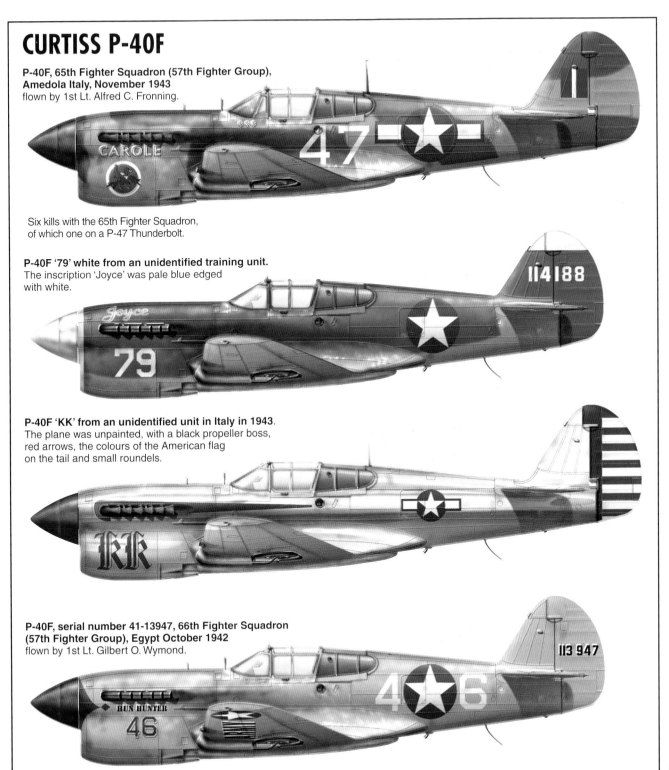

P-40F, 65th Fighter Squadron (57th Fighter Group), Amedola Italy, November 1943
flown by 1st Lt. Alfred C. Fronning.

Six kills with the 65th Fighter Squadron,
of which one on a P-47 Thunderbolt.

P-40F '79' white from an unidentified training unit.
The inscription 'Joyce' was pale blue edged
with white.

P-40F 'KK' from an unidentified unit in Italy in 1943.
The plane was unpainted, with a black propeller boss,
red arrows, the colours of the American flag
on the tail and small roundels.

**P-40F, serial number 41-13947, 66th Fighter Squadron
(57th Fighter Group), Egypt October 1942**
flown by 1st Lt. Gilbert O. Wymond.

CURTISS P-40F

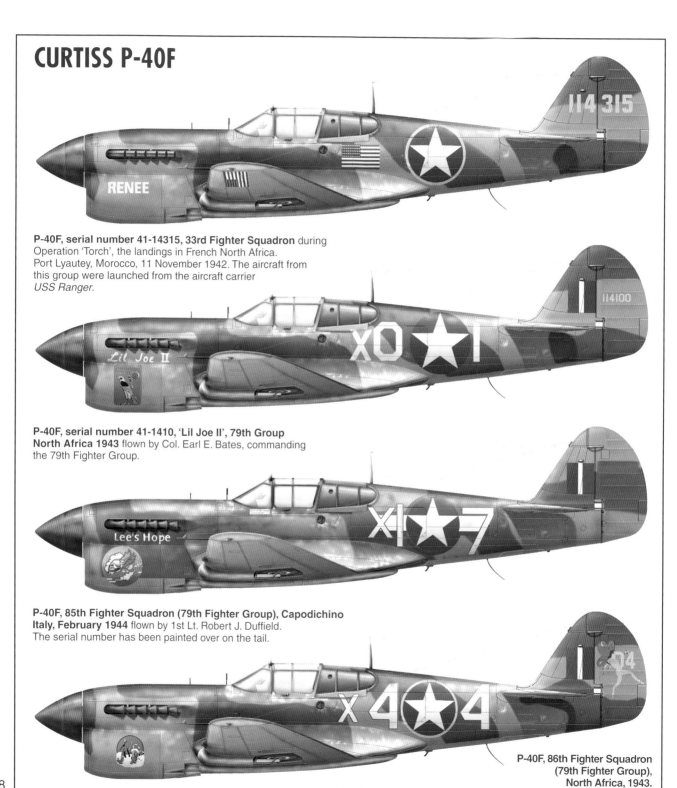

P-40F, serial number 41-14315, 33rd Fighter Squadron during
Operation 'Torch', the landings in French North Africa.
Port Lyautey, Morocco, 11 November 1942. The aircraft from
this group were launched from the aircraft carrier
USS Ranger.

**P-40F, serial number 41-1410, 'Lil Joe II', 79th Group
North Africa 1943** flown by Col. Earl E. Bates, commanding
the 79th Fighter Group.

**P-40F, 85th Fighter Squadron (79th Fighter Group), Capodichino
Italy, February 1944** flown by 1st Lt. Robert J. Duffield.
The serial number has been painted over on the tail.

**P-40F, 86th Fighter Squadron
(79th Fighter Group),
North Africa, 1943.**

CURTISS P-40F

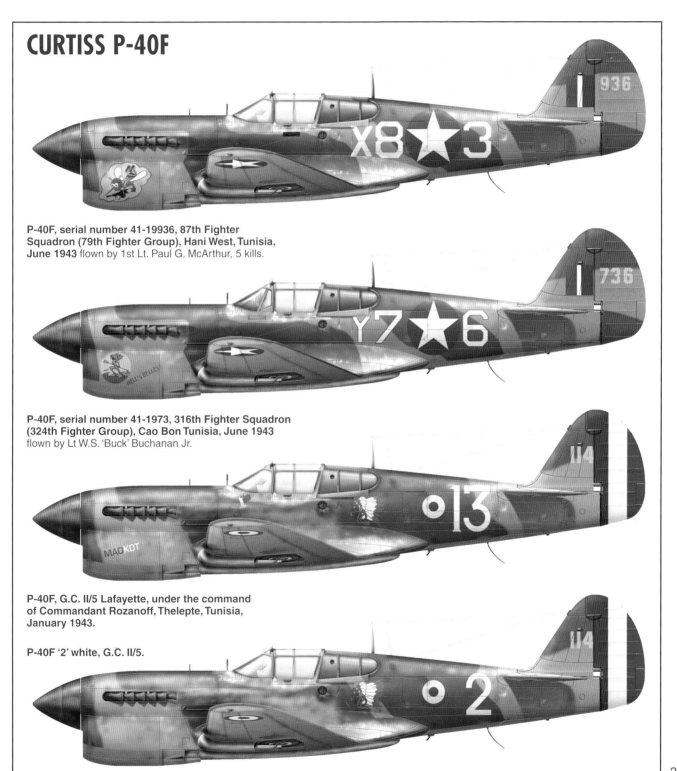

P-40F, serial number 41-19936, 87th Fighter
Squadron (79th Fighter Group), Hani West, Tunisia,
June 1943 flown by 1st Lt. Paul G. McArthur, 5 kills.

P-40F, serial number 41-1973, 316th Fighter Squadron
(324th Fighter Group), Cao Bon Tunisia, June 1943
flown by Lt W.S. 'Buck' Buchanan Jr.

P-40F, G.C. II/5 Lafayette, under the command
of Commandant Rozanoff, Thelepte, Tunisia,
January 1943.

P-40F '2' white, G.C. II/5.

CURTISS P-40F

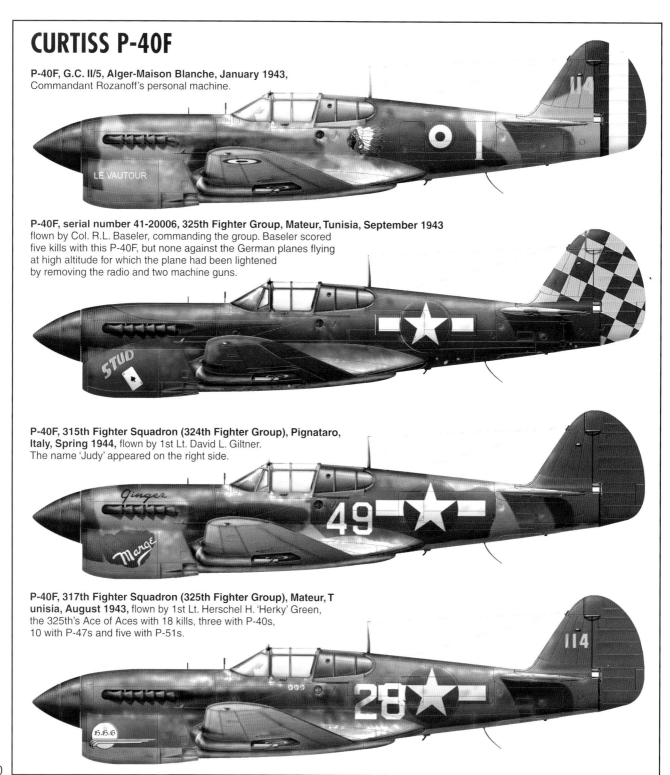

P-40F, G.C. II/5, Alger-Maison Blanche, January 1943,
Commandant Rozanoff's personal machine.

P-40F, serial number 41-20006, 325th Fighter Group, Mateur, Tunisia, September 1943
flown by Col. R.L. Baseler, commanding the group. Baseler scored
five kills with this P-40F, but none against the German planes flying
at high altitude for which the plane had been lightened
by removing the radio and two machine guns.

**P-40F, 315th Fighter Squadron (324th Fighter Group), Pignataro,
Italy, Spring 1944,** flown by 1st Lt. David L. Giltner.
The name 'Judy' appeared on the right side.

**P-40F, 317th Fighter Squadron (325th Fighter Group), Mateur, T
unisia, August 1943,** flown by 1st Lt. Herschel H. 'Herky' Green,
the 325th's Ace of Aces with 18 kills, three with P-40s,
10 with P-47s and five with P-51s.

CURTISS P-40F

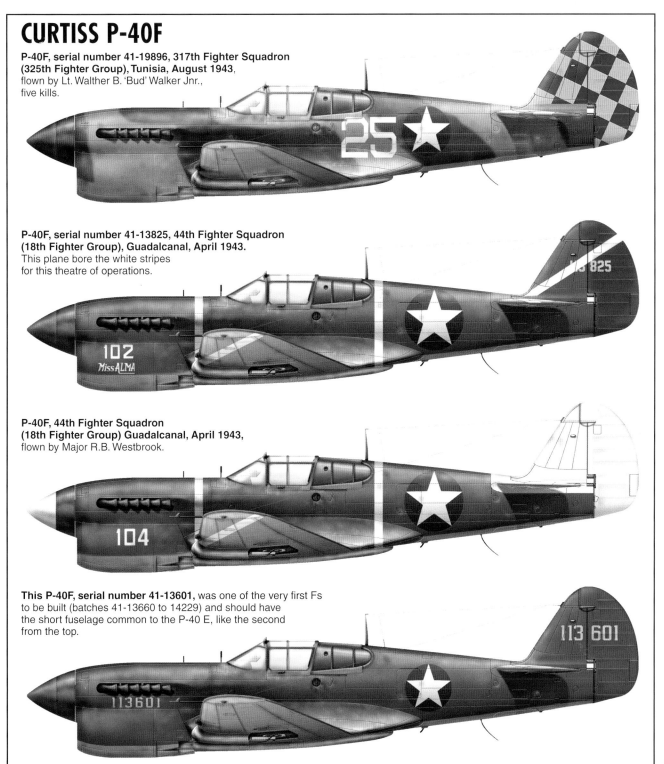

**P-40F, serial number 41-19896, 317th Fighter Squadron
(325th Fighter Group), Tunisia, August 1943**,
flown by Lt. Walther B. 'Bud' Walker Jnr.,
five kills.

**P-40F, serial number 41-13825, 44th Fighter Squadron
(18th Fighter Group), Guadalcanal, April 1943.**
This plane bore the white stripes
for this theatre of operations.

**P-40F, 44th Fighter Squadron
(18th Fighter Group) Guadalcanal, April 1943,**
flown by Major R.B. Westbrook.

This P-40F, serial number 41-13601, was one of the very first Fs
to be built (batches 41-13660 to 14229) and should have
the short fuselage common to the P-40 E, like the second
from the top.

The CURTISS P-40K

This model which appeared in 1942 took up some of the features common to the E and the F. It was fitted this time with an Allison V-1710-73 giving 1325 bhp at take-off, and 1 300 machines were produced for an order signed on October 28, 1941, divided into four lots - 600 P-40K-1CUs (serial numbers 42-45722 to 42-46321), 200 P-40K-5CUs (serial numbers 42-9730 to 42-9929), 335 P-40K-10CU (serial numbers 42-9930 to 42-10264) and 165 P-40K-15 CUs (serial numbers 42-10265 to 42-10429), delivered between May and November 1942, concurrently with the P-40F.

The first 800 examples (P-40K-1/K-5) had the 'E's fuselage to which was added a dorsal fin in front of the tail plane with increased chord in order to try to solve the problem of directional instability, which was aggravated by the increased power of the engine.

This solution was not entirely satisfactory (the Curtiss team never actually sorted this problem out entirely as there was never really any agreement over its causes; some, like D. Berlin, thought that the flow of hot air which formed around the nose air intake (which had to be redesigned) was, in his opinion, responsible and caused turbulence which no dorsal fin between the tail and the fuselage or its extension could eliminate) and the subsequent lots were built from a lengthened P-40F airframe (models P-40K-10/K-15).

Among the innovations based upon this model, there was the XP-40K, built from the P-40K-10 (serial number 42-10219), fitted with an Allison V-1710-43, with a completely redesigned fuselage

A P-40K with a short fuselage (Models K-1 and K-5) before delivery to the RAF, which called it the Kittyhawk Mk III. This version kept the E's fuselage until the K-10s and 15s but with the dorsal fin to improve in-flight performance. (USAF)

in which the very voluminous nose was completely hidden under the belly between the wing leading edges. This attempt was designed to try out a new cooling system; it was not taken up but was used again on the P-40Q.

Another consisted in equipping a P-40K (serial number 42-10181) with a double cockpit without a canopy, with a undercarriage leg mounted on the front to facilitate taxiing for pilots training to use tricycle landing-geared planes.

As with the P-40E and F, some P-40K-15CUs were modified, the openings around the exhaust pipes were sealed for operations in Alaska and in the Aleutians with the 343rd Fighter Group.

The P-40K was mainly operational from the beginning of 1,943in China, Burma and India with the 23rd Fighter Group (14th Air Force) and the 51st Fighter Group (10th and then 14th Air Force from October 1943).

Apart from the planes they received normally, these two groups also received almost a whole Chinese order for 200 machines under the Lend-Lease programme, which were unable to be delivered.

Others joined the Mediterranean theatre of operations with the 57th Fighter Group or New Guinea with the 49th Fighter Group.

British were due to receive an order for 352 machines but only recieved 192 (serial numbers FL 875 to 905, FL-111 to 115, FL-210 to 361, and FL 710 to 713), the rest being returned to the USAAF to be used in North Africa where 112 Squadron RAF was operating on Kittyhawks III.*

The Brazilians also received 25 K-1s as did the Russians and the Canadians, in Alaska and the Aleutians.

*This name from the British designation covered both the P-40K and the P-40M.

(USAAF)

A P-40K, serial number 42-46051, during a test flight as evidenced by its very new look and lack of exhaust marks on the fuselage. The extension of the fin served to compensate for the increase in power from the Allison V-1710-13 for the problem of longitudinal stability.

From the P-40K-10 and 15s onwards, the fuselage got longer as on this example (serial number 42-10343), specially equipped to operate in very harsh, cold climates, thanks to filling in all openings especially the exhaust pipes, and other equipment inside the cockpit. *(DR)*

(DR)

A very beautiful shot of the front of Major Edward M. Nollmeyer's P-40K, 26th Fighter Squadron (51st Fighter Group) at Kunming in China towards the end of 1943. This aircraft had a double yellow stripe around the tail, a white 255 on the tail and American stars edged with red. (USAAF)

Specification for the P-40K

Powerplant
One Allison V-1710-73 rated at 1 325bhp

Dimensions
Wingspan: 37 ft 4 ins (11.38 m)
Length: Standard fuselage: 31 ft 4 ins (9.65 m), **lengthened fuselage:** 33 ft (10.16 m)
Wing surface: 2136 sq. ft.
Height: 12 ft 4 ins (3.76 m)

Weight:
Unloaded: 6 382 lbs (2 901 kg)
Loaded: 8 390 lbs (3814 kg)

Max. All-up weight: 9 988 lbs (4 540 kg)

Performance
Max. Speed: 363 mph (582 kph) at 19 825 ft (6 100 m)
Cruising Speed: 291 mph (467 kph)
Climb Rate: 1 982 ft (610 m) min
Ceiling: 28 548 ft (8 784 m)
Range: 703 miles (1 125 km) or 1 607 miles (2 572 km) with drop tank

Armament
Six 12.7 mm machine guns.

CURTISS P-40K

P-40K, 78th Fighter Squadron (15th/18th Fighter Groups - *the squadron was affected to both groups*)**, Hawaii, 1942-3,** flown by Capt. Gordon Hyde. Camouflage: Dark olive drab, sand and neutral grey.

P-40K, 25th Fighter Squadron (51st Fighter Group), Assam, India 1944. Camouflage was apparently grey, probably sea grey ANA 603 on the upper surfaces and light grey underneath, or medium sea grey and light grey.

P-40K, 75th Fighter Squadron (23rd Fighter Group), China, spring 1943 flown by Capt. John Hampshire Jr., who became the first ace of the 75th Fighter Squadron in November 1942. He died aboard this machine on 2 May 1943

P-40K, 75th Fighter Squadron (23st Fighter Group), China, October 1943 flown by Major Elmer F. Richardson, eight kills. The double white stripe indicates that he was the commanding officer of the 75th Fighter Squadron.

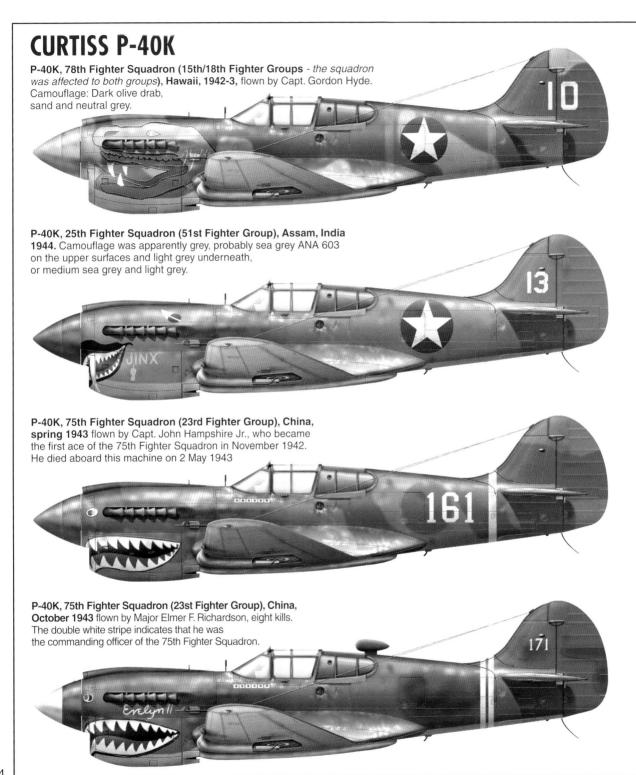

44

CURTISS P-40K

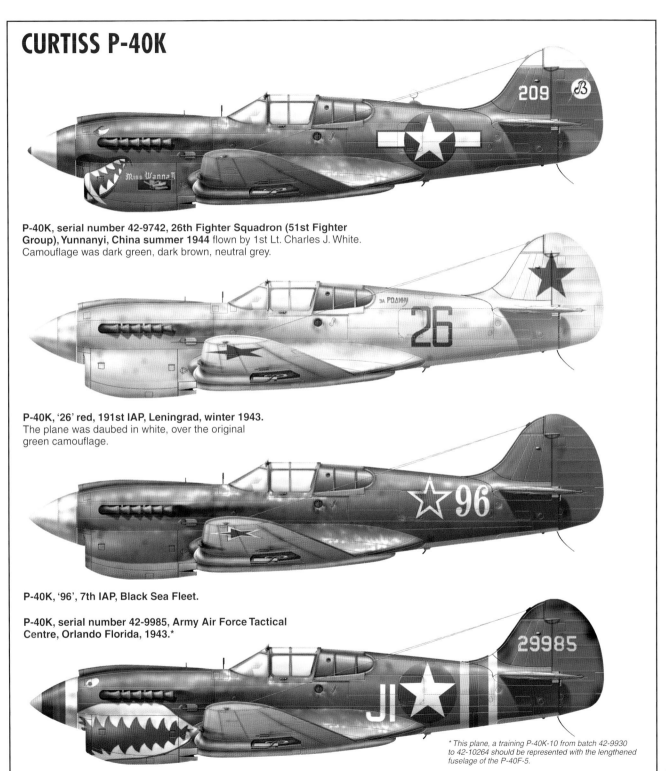

P-40K, serial number 42-9742, 26th Fighter Squadron (51st Fighter Group), Yunnanyi, China summer 1944 flown by 1st Lt. Charles J. White. Camouflage was dark green, dark brown, neutral grey.

P-40K, '26' red, 191st IAP, Leningrad, winter 1943. The plane was daubed in white, over the original green camouflage.

P-40K, '96', 7th IAP, Black Sea Fleet.

P-40K, serial number 42-9985, Army Air Force Tactical Centre, Orlando Florida, 1943.*

* This plane, a training P-40K-10 from batch 42-9930 to 42-10264 should be represented with the lengthened fuselage of the P-40F-5.

CURTISS P-40K

P-40K, 66th Fighter Squadron (57st Fighter Group), Cap Bon Tunisia May 1943, flown by Capt. George W. 'Pop' Long.

P-40K, 23rd Fighter Squadron, Hengyang, China, 1943-44 flown by Lt. Levis. Camouflage was olive drab, neutral grey with perhaps some medium green blotches on the upper surfaces, the tail and the wing tips.

P-40K, '205' white, serial number 42-469140, 78th Fighter Squadron (18th Fighter Group), 1943.

Kittyhawk Mk III, 112 Squadron RAF, Italy, October 1943. Camouflage was dark earth, middle stone, azure blue.

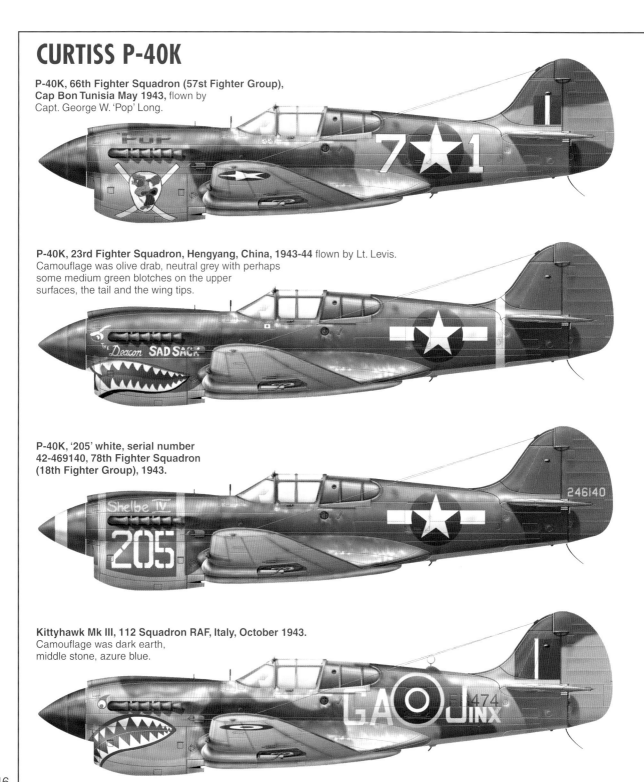

CURTISS P-40K

P-40K, 75th Fighter Squadron (23rd Fighter Group), China, spring 1943 flown by Major Grant Mahony, squadron commander.

The nationality insignia has been hidden olive drab touch up. The double white stripe is on the tail.

P-40K, 26th Fighter Squadron (51st Fighter Group), India, summer 1943 flown by Capt. Charles Caldwell. 'US ARMY' has not been removed from under the wings in spite of the period.

P-40K, 26th Fighter Squadron (51st Fighter Group), Kunming, China, 1943-44.
On this plane the shark's mouth appeared at the beginning of 1944.
Pilot: Major Edward M. Nollmeyer, squadron commander
(indicated by the double yellow stripe), five kills.

Kittyhawk Mk III, EW 421, SAAF, North Africa, 1942.
Pilot: Major D.B. Haupt-Fleisch.

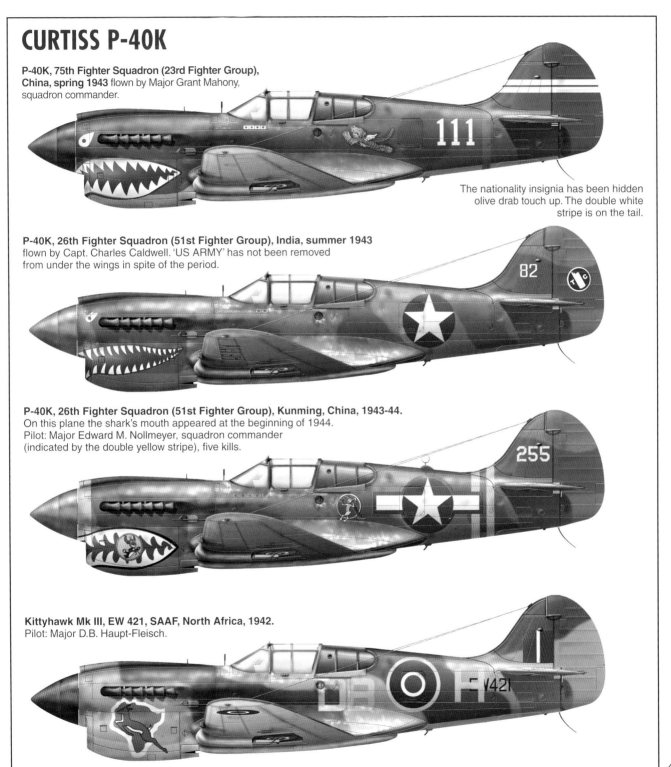

CURTISS P-40K

P-40K, 7th Fighter Squadron (49th Fighter Group), flown by Capt. Frank A. Nichols. The tip of the propeller boss has sometimes been given as red.

P-40K, serial number 42-48217, 78th Fighter Squadron in 1945. Camouflage was sand 26, dark green 30, neutral grey.

P-40K, serial number 42-46046, 64th Fighter Squadron (57th Fighter Group), Hani Main, Tunisia, May 1943, flown by 1st Lt. R Johnson 'Jay' Overcash, 5 kills.

P-40K, 75th Fighter Squadron (23rd Fighter Group), China, spring 1943, flown by 1st Lt. Joseph H. Griffin.

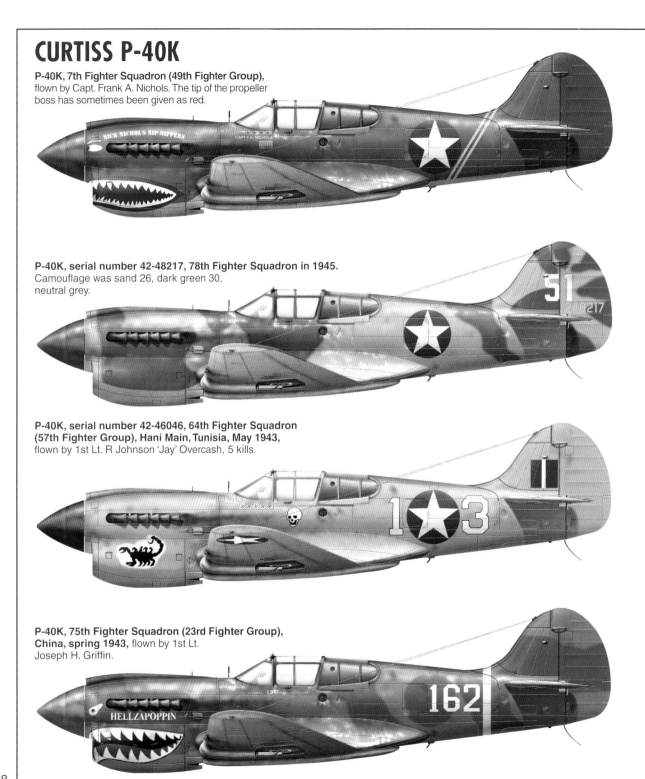

CURTISS P-40K

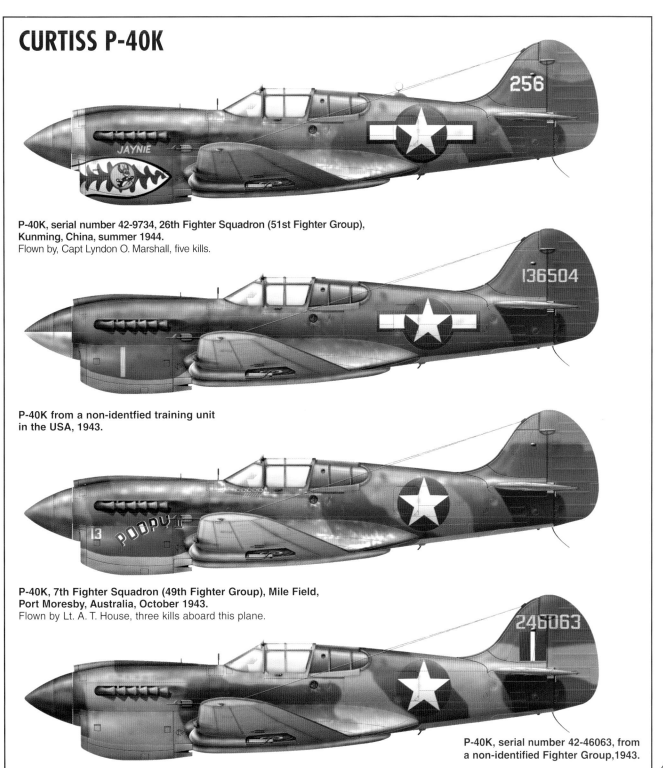

P-40K, serial number 42-9734, 26th Fighter Squadron (51st Fighter Group),
Kunming, China, summer 1944.
Flown by, Capt Lyndon O. Marshall, five kills.

P-40K from a non-identfied training unit
in the USA, 1943.

P-40K, 7th Fighter Squadron (49th Fighter Group), Mile Field,
Port Moresby, Australia, October 1943.
Flown by Lt. A. T. House, three kills aboard this plane.

P-40K, serial number 42-46063, from
a non-identified Fighter Group,1943.

The CURTISS P-40L

With a constant view to improving the performance of the P-40 which had confirmed itself as a robust fighter if albeit not a particularly brilliant one, from the P-40L onwards it was decided to lighten the airframe by removing all that could be removed.

Thus two wing machine guns were removed, the number of rounds was reduced from 280 to 200, 140 litres of fuel capacity was removed -from the wing leading edge tanks - armour protection and equipment were also removed.

The initial fuselage resembled very closely that of the first P-40Fs with the short fuselage (P-40L-1, serial numbers 42-10430 to 42-10479), and the first model kept all its initial armament, i.e. six 12.7 mm machine guns.

It was followed by the P-40L-5CU (42-10480 to 42-10699), of which 220 were produced - they included the reduction in fuel capacity, machine guns and a reduction of 448 lbs (204kgs) owing to lighter armour protection - together with 148 P-40L-10CUs (serial numbers 42-10700 to 42-10847) equipped with improved control systems for the trim and the engine turnover; and 112 P-40L-15CUs (serial numbers 42-10848 to 42-10959) fitted with carburettor filters and different navigation lights; and finally 170 P-40L -20CUs (serial numbers 42-10960 to 42-11129) with redesigned electric and radio equipment, the SCR-695 which had a system for blocking the friend-foe identification equipment.

From the P-40L-5CU onwards, all the planes were made with the P-40F's 18-inch extended fuselage and a small ventilation panel was put into the left hand side of the cockpit windshield, a small detail which permits a P-40F to be distinguished from an L.

The engine was the Merlin Packard V-1650, but in spite of this, the speed increase was negligible, barely 5 miles per hour faster. The pilots called this version, which was delivered in the first four months of 1943, 'Gipsy Rose Lee' after a nude dancer who was famous at the time. It goes without saying that the reduced armament did nothing to increase the model's credibility.

It was originally destined for the Allied air forces under Lend-Lease and equipped a number of American units serving in North Africa, especially the 99th Fighter Squadron (323rd Fighter Group) which was

A P-40L-5, serial number 42-10554 which was part of the first batch (220 produced) of P-40Ls built with a lengthened fuselage before delivery . The upper air intake has been removed on this lightened version of the P-40F fitted with a Packard V-1650, based on the British Rolls Royce. The bottom of the tail has not been painted and the chalk marks on the fuselage show that the radio installation has been completed successfully. Note the twin-engined Douglas A-20 Havoc, in the background partly hidden. (DR)

entirely made up of coloured personnel. The British received 100 (this figure is to be treated with caution as the sources disagree where deliveries are concerned because of the RAF's own numbering system and because of the numerous machines returned to the Americans and the Commonwealth) examples of this model called the Kittyhawk II (serials FS 400 to 499) which were operational in North Africa, their main theatre of operations alongside the P-40F.

Production ceased, as for the P-40F, with the fitting of an Allison V-1710 engine instead of the Packard Merlin V-1650 (the new P-51B Mustang was being given priority) onto 53 P-40Ls, which were then re-designated P-40R-1CU and given over to training.

P-40L-20 during a test flight in the USA. Total production of the P-40F ended at the end of spring 1943, after 700 examples had been built.
(DR)

A training flight in the USA with a P-40K, P-40F and P-40L flying together. The P-40L is recognisable by its four wing mounted machine guns instead of the usual six. The '3' yellow is serial number 42-10516 which means that it was a P-401L-5.
(USAF)

Specification for the P-40L

Powerplant
One Packard V-1650 (Rolls-Royce Merlin 28 built under licence) rated at 1 300bhp.

Dimensions
Wingspan: 37 ft 4 ins (11.38 m)
Length: Standard fuselage: 31 ft 4 ins (9.65 m), **lengthened fuselage:** 33 ft (10.16 m)
Wing surface: 2136 sq. ft.
Height: 12 ft 4 ins (3.76 m)

Weight
Unloaded: 6 470 lbs (2 941kg)

Max. All-up weight: 8 377 lbs (3 808kg)

Performance
Max. Speed: 371 mph (595 kph) at 19,825ft (6,100m)
Cruising Speed: 251 mph (402kph)
Climb Rate: 3 276 ft/min (1 008 m/min)
Ceiling: 38 550 ft (11 800 m)
Range: 653 miles (1,045km), 1 390 miles (2 221 km) with drop tank

Armament
Four 12.7 mm machine guns.

The same plane shown in a training unit in the USA during 1943. The insignia behind the American star has not been clearly identified and could be red on a white background. The plane has been painted olive drab and neutral grey with the tail plane serial number painted yellow.
(DR)

51

CURTISS P-40L

P-40L, serial number 42-10653, 324th Fighter Group, Cercola, Italy, December 1943 flown by Col. William K. 'Sandy' Bates, commanding the group.

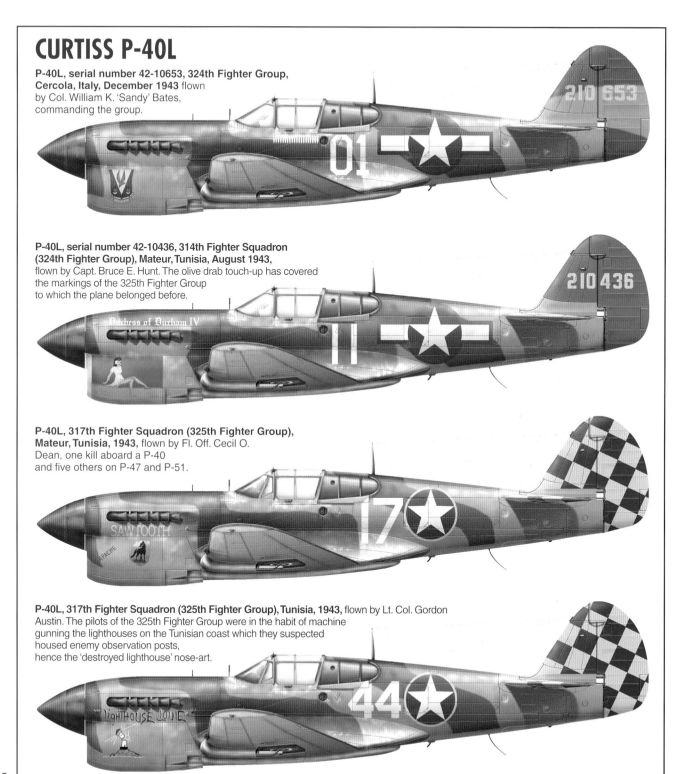

P-40L, serial number 42-10436, 314th Fighter Squadron (324th Fighter Group), Mateur, Tunisia, August 1943, flown by Capt. Bruce E. Hunt. The olive drab touch-up has covered the markings of the 325th Fighter Group to which the plane belonged before.

P-40L, 317th Fighter Squadron (325th Fighter Group), Mateur, Tunisia, 1943, flown by Fl. Off. Cecil O. Dean, one kill aboard a P-40 and five others on P-47 and P-51.

P-40L, 317th Fighter Squadron (325th Fighter Group), Tunisia, 1943, flown by Lt. Col. Gordon Austin. The pilots of the 325th Fighter Group were in the habit of machine gunning the lighthouses on the Tunisian coast which they suspected housed enemy observation posts, hence the 'destroyed lighthouse' nose-art.

CURTISS P-40L

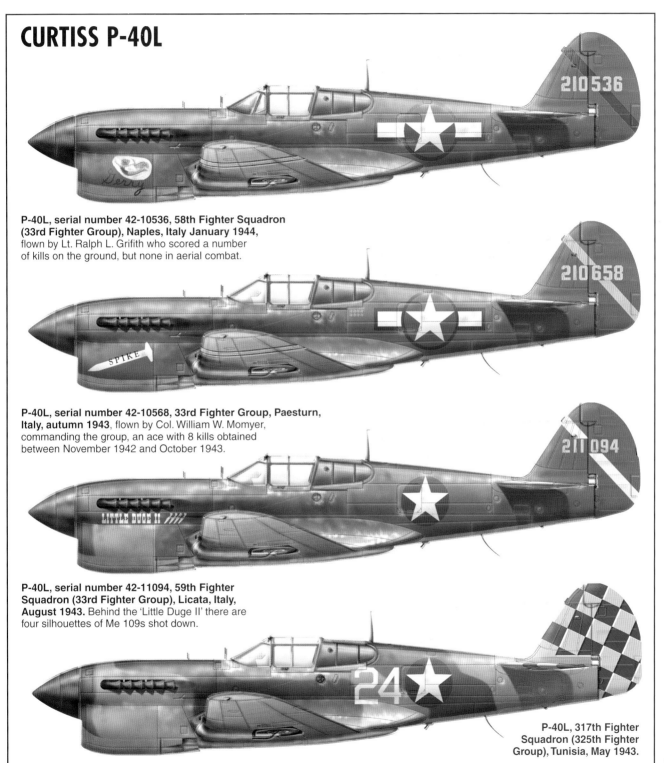

P-40L, serial number 42-10536, 58th Fighter Squadron (33rd Fighter Group), Naples, Italy January 1944, flown by Lt. Ralph L. Grifith who scored a number of kills on the ground, but none in aerial combat.

P-40L, serial number 42-10568, 33rd Fighter Group, Paesturn, Italy, autumn 1943, flown by Col. William W. Momyer, commanding the group, an ace with 8 kills obtained between November 1942 and October 1943.

P-40L, serial number 42-11094, 59th Fighter Squadron (33rd Fighter Group), Licata, Italy, August 1943. Behind the 'Little Duge II' there are four silhouettes of Me 109s shot down.

P-40L, 317th Fighter Squadron (325th Fighter Group), Tunisia, May 1943.

53

CURTISS P-40L

P-40L, serial number 42-10855, 99th Fighter Squadron (79th Fighter Group), Capodichino, Italy, January 1944,
flown by 1st Lt. Robert W. Deiz.

P-40L, 319th Fighter Squadron (325th Fighter Group), Tunisia, May 1943. The 319th Fighter Squadron was credited with 36 confirmed kills during its tour of operations in the Mediterranean sector, April to October 1943.

P-40L, serial number 42-10866, headquarters of the 325th Fighter Group, Mateur, Tunisia, September 1943
flown by John C.A. Watkins, who died in a P-47 after a bad weather crash.

P-40L, serial number 42-10664, 316th Fighter Squadron (324th Fighter Group), Cercola, Italy,
spring 1944 flown by Major Paul T.O. Pizzi Jr., commanding the 316th Fighter squadron.
This machine had come from the 325th Fighter Group as the olive drab touch up shows and had red wheel discs.

CURTISS P-40L

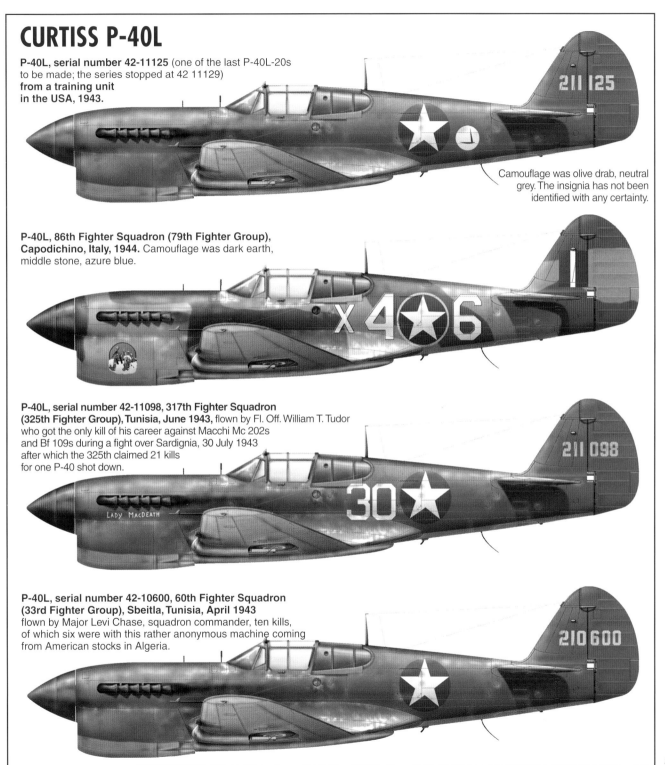

P-40L, serial number 42-11125 (one of the last P-40L-20s to be made; the series stopped at 42 11129) **from a training unit in the USA, 1943.**

Camouflage was olive drab, neutral grey. The insignia has not been identified with any certainty.

P-40L, 86th Fighter Squadron (79th Fighter Group), Capodichino, Italy, 1944. Camouflage was dark earth, middle stone, azure blue.

P-40L, serial number 42-11098, 317th Fighter Squadron (325th Fighter Group), Tunisia, June 1943, flown by Fl. Off. William T. Tudor who got the only kill of his career against Macchi Mc 202s and Bf 109s during a fight over Sardignia, 30 July 1943 after which the 325th claimed 21 kills for one P-40 shot down.

P-40L, serial number 42-10600, 60th Fighter Squadron (33rd Fighter Group), Sbeitla, Tunisia, April 1943 flown by Major Levi Chase, squadron commander, ten kills, of which six were with this rather anonymous machine coming from American stocks in Algeria.

CURTISS P-40L

P-40L, serial number 42-10857, 86th Fighter Squadron (79th Fighter Group), Capodichino, Italy, January 1944,
flown by Lt. Michael Mauritz.
This plane remained underwater off Capo Portiere in Italy for 44 years following sabotage, before being lifted out ou restored and exhibited in the Battle of Anzio Museum at Piana delle Orme.
Certain features are to be noted like the fine red edge to the underside roundel, the English fin-flash and its white and yellow registration number. The white 49 on the fuselage was copied on the wheel discs.

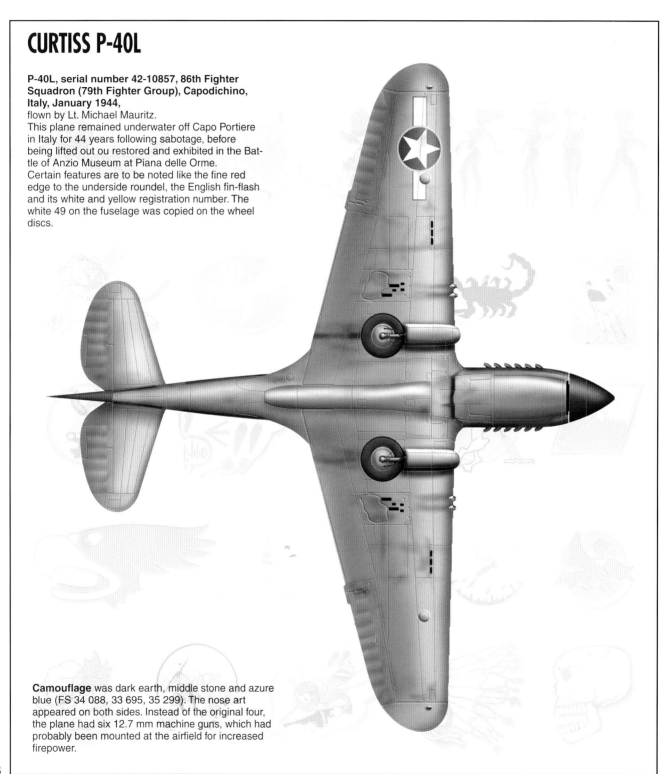

Camouflage was dark earth, middle stone and azure blue (FS 34 088, 33 695, 35 299). The nose art appeared on both sides. Instead of the original four, the plane had six 12.7 mm machine guns, which had probably been mounted at the airfield for increased firepower.

CURTISS P-40L

P-40L, serial number 42-10857, 86th Fighter Squadron (79th Fighter Group), Capodichino, Italy, January 1944, flown by Lt. Michael Mauritz.

The CURTISS P-40M

Among the many models which were delivered first to the Allied nations, the production of the P-40M unlike that of the other versions, was almost entirely delivered to its original purchasers. The M kept the lengthened fuselage of the L and was fitted with an Allison V-171-81 1200bhp engine. In order to cool it, two small rectangular fifteen-hole panels were placed in front of the exhaust pipes, which were found on the P-40R (fitted with the above Allison engines).

600 machines were built and delivered in the following lots: 60 P-40M-1CUs (serial numbers 43-5403 to 43-5462) with reinforced ailerons; 260 P-40M-5CUs (serials 43-5463 to 43-5722) equipped with new carburettor filters and new ailerons; and finally 280 P-40M-10CU (serial numbers 43-5723 to 43-6002) which had red indicators on the wings to show that the undercarriage was down and locked, identical to those on the German Fw 190s.

Other modifications inside the cockpit helped to differentiate the P-40M such as the condensation elimination demist system and the fuel pressure gauge.

Overall performance was improved by the (relative) lightening of the machine's airframe, whose weight went down to 8 888lbs (4 040kg) but this improvement was barely noticeable.

Almost all the production of the machines, 595 examples, were delivered between November 1942 and February 1943 to the RAF who gave them the name Kittyhawk III, just like the P-40Ks.

The RAF kept 94 machines (serial numbers FR- 779 to 872) and sent the rest as it often did, to the countries of the Commonwealth (168 machines to Australia and others to No 5 Squadron SAAF in

A P-40M, 44th Fighter squadron (48th Fighter Group) in the Solomon Islands, during the summer of 1943. The M Model was the first of the P-40s to have a small rectangular grill behind the propeller boss, to cool the engine. (USAF)

Italy), to the USSR (170 Machines numbered FS-100 to 269), Brazil (19 machines) who wanted to take part in the allied war effort.

The USAAF sent some to the Far East theatre (India) and the Pacific (Solomon Islands) and others were used for training in the USA.

P-40M-5 (serial number 43-5540) being evaluated in Russia for the Experimental Centre of the Soviet Air Force. (DR)

One of the easiest ways of telling a P-40M from an N since both have a lengthened fuselage and a little grill in front of the exhaust pipe, was the cockpit canopy which on the M remained the same with the rear part still rounded, whereas on the N (except for the first 400 N-1s built (serial numbers 42-104429 to 42-104828) the canopy was squarer which gave better visibility and covered the back part of the cockpit of the aircraft completely. (DR)

Specification for the P-40M

Powerplant
One Allison V-171-81 rated at 1 200bhp for take-off and 1 125bhp at 17 225 feet (5,300m).

Dimensions
Wingspan: 37 ft 4 ins (11.38 m)
Length: 33 ft 4ins (10.16 m)
Wing surface: 236 sq. ft. (22 m²)
Height: 12 ft 4ins (3.76 m)

Weight
Unloaded: 6 454lbs (2 934kgs)
Max. All-up Weight: 8 888lbs (4 040kg)

Performance
Max. Speed: 362 mph at 19 825 ft 579kph at 6 100 m) and 356 mph at 24 700 ft (570kph at 7 600 m)
Cruising Speed: 290 mph (466kph)
Climb Rate: 2 035 ft/min (626 m/min)
Ceiling: 29 740 ft (9 150 m)
Range: 703 miles (1 125 km), 1 607 miles (2 572 km) with drop tank

Armament
Six 12.7 mm machine guns

CURTISS P-40M

P-40M, 25th Fighter Squadron (51st Fighter Group), Yunnanyi, China, Summer 1944, flown by Capt. Paul S. Royer, three kills of which two were confirmed.

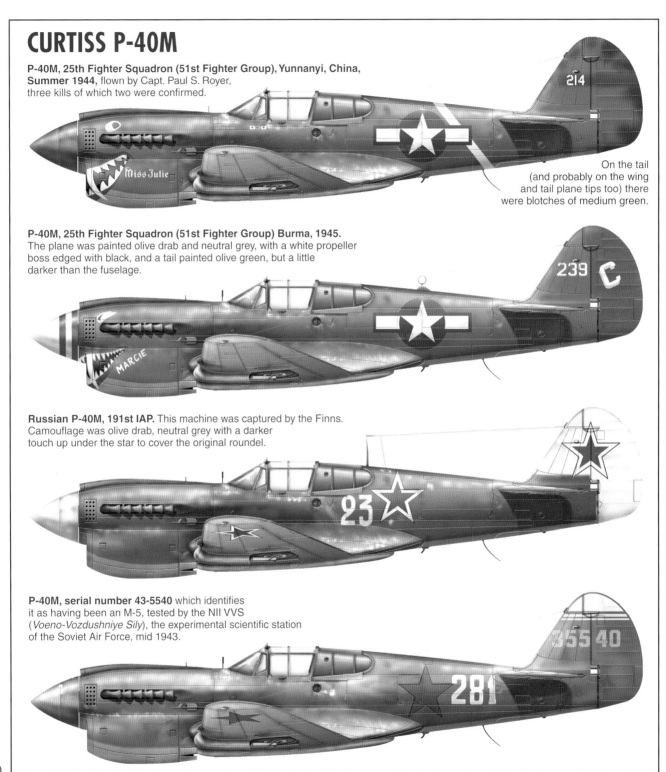

On the tail (and probably on the wing and tail plane tips too) there were blotches of medium green.

P-40M, 25th Fighter Squadron (51st Fighter Group) Burma, 1945. The plane was painted olive drab and neutral grey, with a white propeller boss edged with black, and a tail painted olive green, but a little darker than the fuselage.

Russian P-40M, 191st IAP. This machine was captured by the Finns. Camouflage was olive drab, neutral grey with a darker touch up under the star to cover the original roundel.

P-40M, serial number 43-5540 which identifies it as having been an M-5, tested by the NII VVS (*Voeno-Vozdushniye Sily*), the experimental scientific station of the Soviet Air Force, mid 1943.

CURTISS P-40M

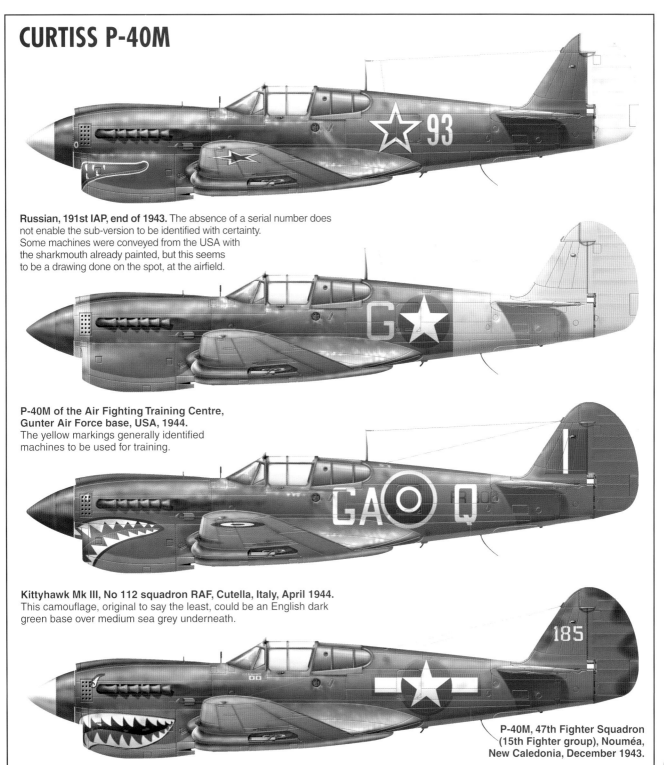

Russian, 191st IAP, end of 1943. The absence of a serial number does not enable the sub-version to be identified with certainty. Some machines were conveyed from the USA with the sharkmouth already painted, but this seems to be a drawing done on the spot, at the airfield.

P-40M of the Air Fighting Training Centre, Gunter Air Force base, USA, 1944. The yellow markings generally identified machines to be used for training.

Kittyhawk Mk III, No 112 squadron RAF, Cutella, Italy, April 1944. This camouflage, original to say the least, could be an English dark green base over medium sea grey underneath.

P-40M, 47th Fighter Squadron (15th Fighter group), Nouméa, New Caledonia, December 1943.

The CURTISS P-40N

This was the model which was produced in the greatest numbers; 5 220 were built. It was the last attempt made by Curtiss to give this old plane a second youth.

Although the USAAF was in a position to receive a large quantity of more modern aircraft, it asked Curtiss to maintain its production capacity to take advantage of the shorter development time and to continue to supply the beneficiaries of the Lend- Lease agreement, especially the USSR.

Efforts were made to lighten the airframe, as on the P-40L: the 546-litre leading-edge tanks were removed, two wing-mounted machine guns were removed, smaller tyres equipped with magnesium wheel discs (which were more often than not removed) were fitted, new aluminium (a much lighter metal) radiators were designed, the internal battery was removed at first but later kept on production models as this was satisfactory. The aircraft was powered by an Allison V-1710-81 which enabled the plane whose weight was now around 7 700lbs (3 500kgs) in its combat configuration, to reach 375 mph (600kph) at 10 460 feet (3 200 m).

A first batch of 400 aircraft was built, P-40N-1CUs (serial numbers 42-104429 to 42-104828) which were delivered between March and April 1943. As from the next batch of 1100 P-40N-5CUs (serial numbers 42-104829 to 42 105928), delivered from May to July 1943, there was a new cockpit canopy which was to become the distinctive feature of the P-40N. It was a single piece which had wide lower angled supports, and the glass section behind and above the pilot's armour plating section was deeper now and ended at right angles under the antenna mast in order to improve rearward visibility.

There was a new type of seat and an SCR 696 radio. Armament was standard again, since the reduced version was not satisfactory. The wings were at last given pylons for drop tanks or 500 lb (227 kg) bombs.

With the P-40N-10CU (100 examples built, serial numbers 42-105929 to 42-106028, delivered in August 1943), there were only four machine guns, as the plane had been optimised for use in harsh climates. On the P-400N-15 of which 377 were produced and delivered in September 1943, serial numbers 42-106029 to 42-106405), the six 12.7 mm machine guns had been reinstalled

This P-40N is one of the most photographed machines of this version, having had the privilege of being the 15 000th Curtiss fighter built. For the occasion it wore the flags of all the Buffalo firm's customers. *(DR)*

Specifications for the P-40N

Powerplant
One Allison V-171-81/99/115 rated at between 1 200bhp and 1 360bhp.

Dimensions
Wingspan: 37 ft 4 ins (11.38 m)
Length: (longer fuselage) 33 ft 4ins (10.16 m), (shorter fuselage) 31 ft 4 ins (9.65 m)
Wing surface: 236 sq. ft. (22 m²)
Height: 12 ft 4ins (3.76 m)

Weight
Unloaded: 6 000 lbs (2 724 kg)
Max. All-up Weight: 7788 lbs (3 540 kg)

Performance
Max. Speed: 380 mph (608 kph) for the N-1 quipped with four wing mounted machine guns.
Cruising Speed: 284 mph (454kph)
Climb Rate: 2 106 ft/min (648 m/min)
Ceiling: 33 000ft (10 163 m)
Range: 753 miles (1 206 km), 1 406 miles (2 251 km) with drop tank

Armament
Four or six 12.7 mm machine guns, 100 lb and 20 lb bombs under the fuselage and the wings.

This P-40N is an N converted into a two-seat trainer for pilots before being transferred to active units. Forward vision was obtained thanks to the system mounted on the rear canopy support. *(USAF)*

(the pilots had not stopped crying out desperately for them) and wing tank fuel capacity was increased.

The next model, the P-40N-20CU (serial numbers 42-106406 to 42-106428, 43-22752 to 43-24251) of which 1 523 were made between September and December 1943, making it the most numerous of the N sub-variants, was marked by the fitting of an Allison V-1710-99 engine equipped with a new variable pressurisation system. Its bomb load increased to three 500 lb (227kg) bombs.

The machines produced between January and November 1944 were P-40N-25CUs (serial numbers 43-24252 to 43-24751, 500 machines) with self-sealing tanks, a redesigned instrument panel; 500 P-40N-30CUs (serial numbers 44-7001 to 44-7500) with a redesigned oil system; 500 P-40N-35 (serial numbers 44-7501 to 44-8000) which had new instruments, new carburettor systems and radio equipment; and finally 220 P-40N-40CUs (serial numbers 44-47749 to 44-47968) with an Allison V-1710-115 engine fitted with automatic power boost and propeller pitch systems, a redesigned cockpit oxygen supply, new exhaust pipes and all-metal tail fins on the last hundred models.

Among the original P-40s, it is worth mentioning the P-40N-6, -16 and -26s (taken from the N-5,-15 and -25s) which were equipped with reconnaissance cameras in the fuselage; the XP-40N (43-24571) which experimented with tear-drop canopies; the 30 TP-40N two-seat dual-control trainers equipped with a forward viewing system for the instructor sitting behind the pupil; and finally a P-40N-15 (42-106129) fitted with skis.

P-40N-30 (serial number 44 7138), being evaluated before delivery. This shot enables one to see the medium green touch-ups to the wings and the tail surfaces which make it less visible from above.
(USAAF)

A last attempt to improve the performances of the P-40 was made with the XP-40Q equipped with a new Allison 1 425 bhp engine. The airframe used for this was that of a P-40K (42-9987) which was redesigned by moving the lower air intake inside the fuselage between the undercarriage legs.

Various trials led to the definitive version, the XP-40Q-3 (not unlike the P-51 Mustang with its well-shaped air intake under the nose and its teardrop canopy) which reached the speed of 425 mph (680 km) at 20 300feet (6,250m). The armament was to have been the six 12.7 mm machine guns, but these could be replaced by four 20 mm cannon. In spite of such a promising performance, no orders were placed.

Curtiss never really got over this failure which started it on its long decline.

The P-40N served mainly in the Far East, more recent planes like the P-38, P-47 and P-51 being used first in the European theatre of which was the Allies primary objective.

It was to be found being used by the famous 49th and 80th Fighter Groups in New Guinea and India from 1943, in China by the 23rd and 51st Fighter Groups where it protected the supply routes across the Himalayas. In the Aleutian Islands, it equipped the 343rd Fighter Group of the 11th Air Forcce until the end of the conflict. The RAF received a batch of 458 P-40Ns (called Kittyhawk Mk IVs) which equipped No 120 Squadron which was entirely made up of Dutch personnel and operating from December 1943 out of Merauke in New Guinea.

The New Zealanders committed their 172 machines alongside the Americans during the recapture of the Pacific Islands; the Australians used their eight fighter squadrons in New Guinea, Indonesia, Borneo and the Russians received 130 machines.

In Europe, it was used particularly by No 112 Squadron, RAF and No 450 Squadron SAAF in Italy.

CURTISS P-40N

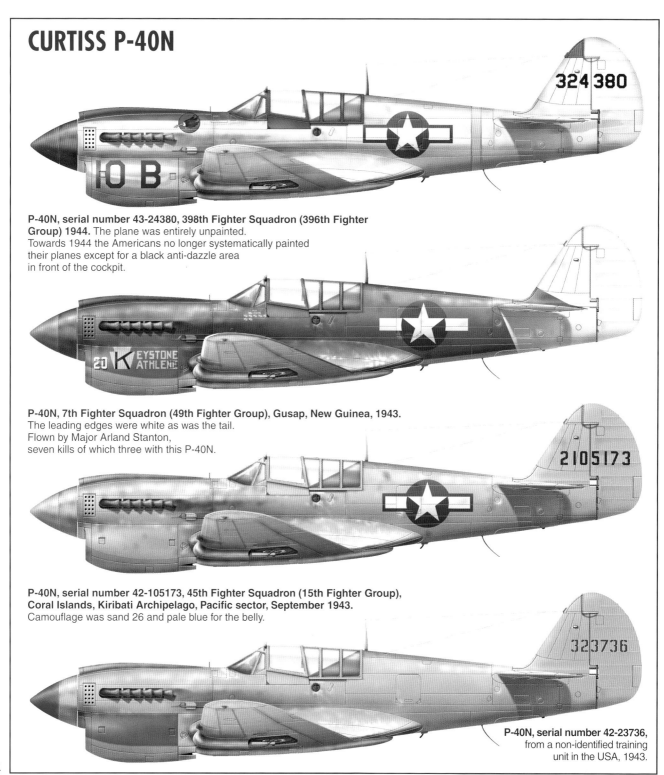

P-40N, serial number 43-24380, 398th Fighter Squadron (396th Fighter Group) 1944. The plane was entirely unpainted.
Towards 1944 the Americans no longer systematically painted their planes except for a black anti-dazzle area in front of the cockpit.

P-40N, 7th Fighter Squadron (49th Fighter Group), Gusap, New Guinea, 1943.
The leading edges were white as was the tail.
Flown by Major Arland Stanton,
seven kills of which three with this P-40N.

P-40N, serial number 42-105173, 45th Fighter Squadron (15th Fighter Group), Coral Islands, Kiribati Archipelago, Pacific sector, September 1943.
Camouflage was sand 26 and pale blue for the belly.

P-40N, serial number 42-23736, from a non-identified training unit in the USA, 1943.

CURTISS P-40N

P-40N, 18th Fighter Squadron (51st Fighter Group),
China, summer 1944, flown by 1st Lt Carl E. Hardy.

The serial number of the
aircraft has been hidden by a
dark green stripe, probably
painted on the airfield.

P-40N, 74th Fighter Squadron (23rd Fighter Group), Kandchow, China, 1944,
flown by 1st Lt. John W. Bolard. This machine was transferred from
the 91st Fighter Squadron (80th Fighter Group) but kept its white
tail markings. Camouflage was olive drab
and neutral grey.

P-40N, 8th Fighter Squadron (49th Fighter Group), Mailian, New Guinea, end of 1943,
flown by Capt. Robert H. Wright. The white for the theatre
of operations has been transferred
to the leading edges of the wings.

P-40N, 8th Fighter Squadron (49th Fighter Group), Gusap, June 1944.
Flown by Lt. Marion Felts. This plane had its original olive drab removed
after an accident and subsequent repairs; it only kept the yellow 45
on the green background. The tail is white which continues under
the American roundel for better visibility.

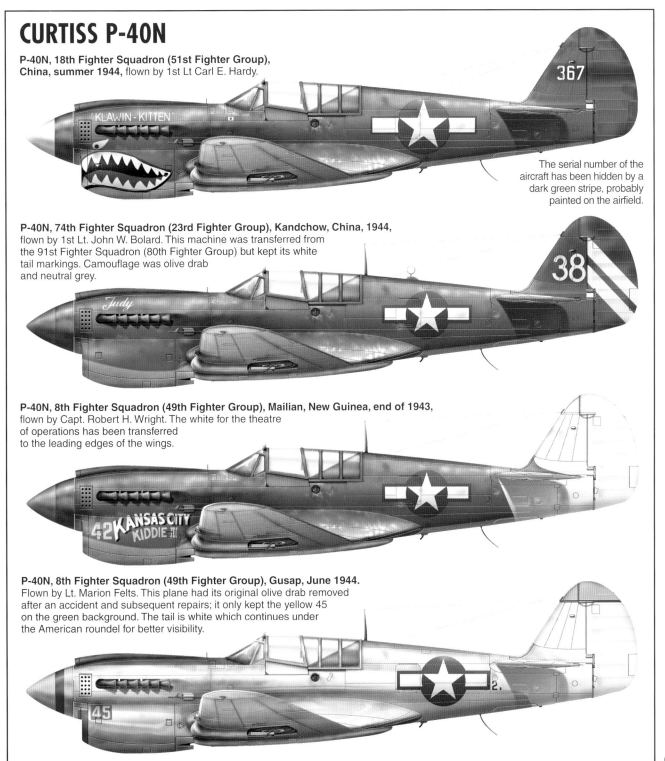

CURTISS P-40N

P-40N, 87th Fighter Squadron (49th Fighter Group), Gusap, New Guinea, February 1944, flown by Lt. Don Meuten, six victories. Camouflage was olive drab, neutral grey.

P-40N, 8th Fighter Squadron (49th Fighter Group), New Guinea, 1943. Flown by Lt. Sammy Pierce. The orange stripe meant that this pilot was a flight leader in the 8th Fighter Squadron which went over from P-40Es to P-40Ns in June 1943. The inscription reads *'KAY, THE STRAWBERRY BLONDE'* and was more of an ivory colour, according to the pilot.

P-40N, 89th Fighter Squadron (80th Fighter Group), Assam, India, spring 1944, flown by 2nd Lt. Herbert H. Doughty. Although it was a P-40N-1, theoretically fitted with four machine guns to gain weight, this plane had six. The red propeller boss indicates that it belonged to the 89th Fighter Squadron.

P-40N, 89th Fighter Squadron (80th Fighter Group), India, spring 1944. The 80th's skull emblem sometimes gave some interesting variations like these two jaw bones and eye of a shark, which is no doubt due to the upper panel being replaced following an accident. The same can be said for the maintenance hatch on the roundel.

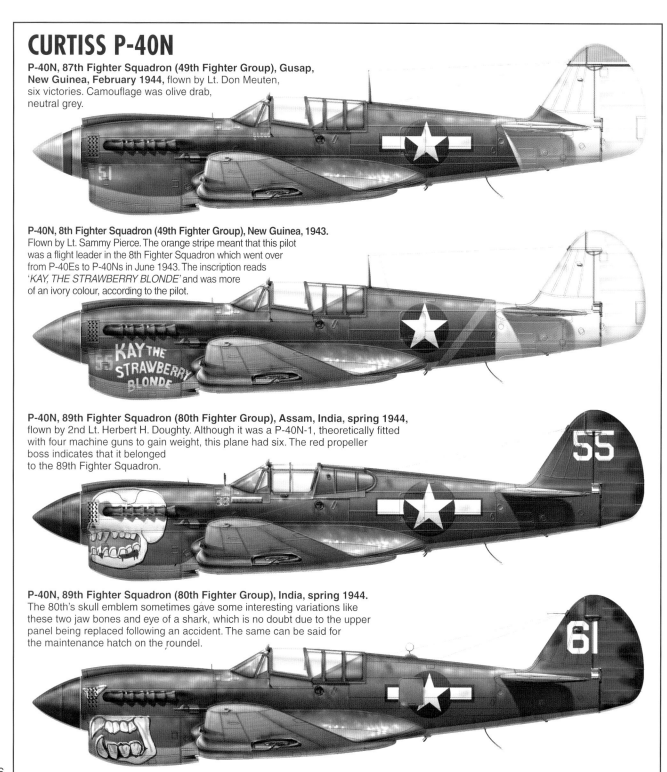

CURTISS P-40N

P-40N, 7th Fighter Squadron (3rd Fighter Group), Laohow, China, January 1945,
flown by Wang Kuang Fu, a veteran of C.L. Chennault's
American Volunteer Group, and an ace of the Chinese
Air Force, with 6.5 victories. Camouflage
was olive drab and neutral grey.

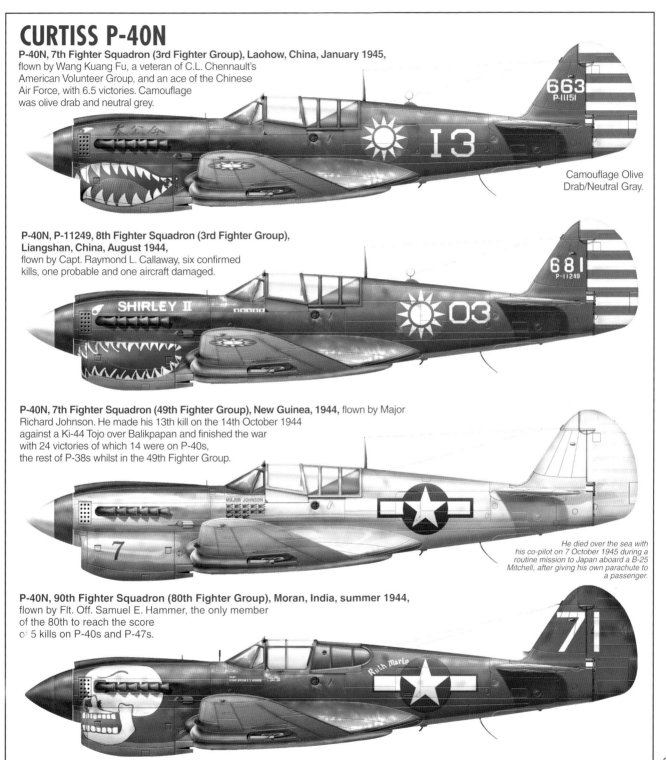

Camouflage Olive
Drab/Neutral Gray.

**P-40N, P-11249, 8th Fighter Squadron (3rd Fighter Group),
Liangshan, China, August 1944,**
flown by Capt. Raymond L. Callaway, six confirmed
kills, one probable and one aircraft damaged.

P-40N, 7th Fighter Squadron (49th Fighter Group), New Guinea, 1944, flown by Major
Richard Johnson. He made his 13th kill on the 14th October 1944
against a Ki-44 Tojo over Balikpapan and finished the war
with 24 victories of which 14 were on P-40s,
the rest of P-38s whilst in the 49th Fighter Group.

*He died over the sea with
his co-pilot on 7 October 1945 during a
routine mission to Japan aboard a B-25
Mitchell, after giving his own parachute to
a passenger.*

P-40N, 90th Fighter Squadron (80th Fighter Group), Moran, India, summer 1944,
flown by Flt. Off. Samuel E. Hammer, the only member
of the 80th to reach the score
of 5 kills on P-40s and P-47s.

CURTISS P-40N

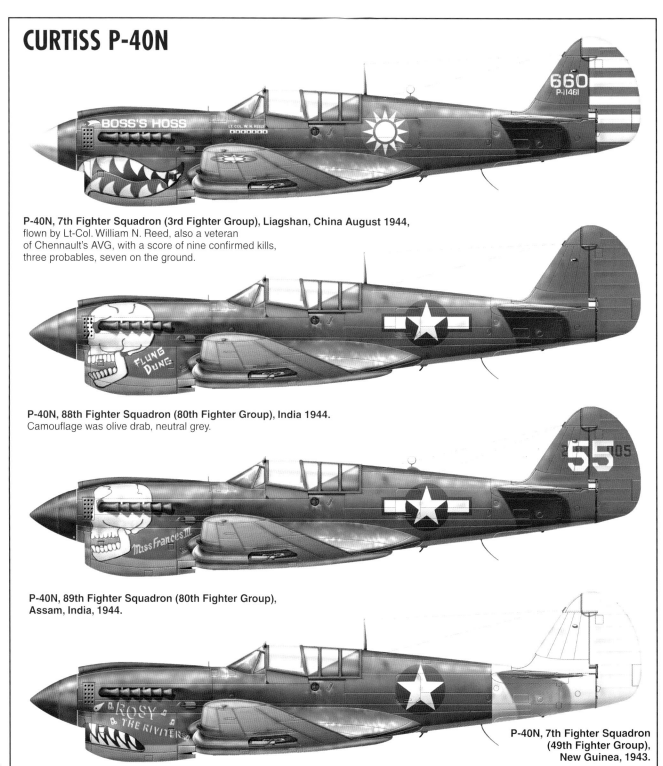

P-40N, 7th Fighter Squadron (3rd Fighter Group), Liagshan, China August 1944,
flown by Lt-Col. William N. Reed, also a veteran
of Chennault's AVG, with a score of nine confirmed kills,
three probables, seven on the ground.

P-40N, 88th Fighter Squadron (80th Fighter Group), India 1944.
Camouflage was olive drab, neutral grey.

P-40N, 89th Fighter Squadron (80th Fighter Group),
Assam, India, 1944.

**P-40N, 7th Fighter Squadron
(49th Fighter Group),
New Guinea, 1943.**

CURTISS P-40N

Kittyhawk Mk IV, No 122 Squadron RAF, flown by Flight
Sergeant G.F.Davis, Cutella, Italy, April 1944.
Camouflaged with dark earth,
middle stone and azure blue.

**P-40N, serial number 42-105202, 7th Fighter Squadron (49th Fighter Group),
New Guinea, January 1944**, flown by Lt. Bob DeHaven,
fourteen kills. The orchid is sometimes given as pink, whereas
the leading edges were normally white.

**P-40N, serial number 42-105112, 45th Fighter Squadron (15thFighter Group), Nanuméa Islands, Pacific
Ocean., December 1943,** flown by Lt. Bruce Campbell. Camouflage was
sand 26 (FS 34133) on blue or pale grey. The colours of the machines
in the 45th Fighter Squadron are still under debate and some have given
the upper surfaces as being pale grey
(USN light grey FS 36440).

**P-40N, serial number 43-23194, 7th Fighter Squadron (49th Fighter
Group), Middleburg Islands, New Guinea, 1944.**
The plane was unpainted with white tail planes.

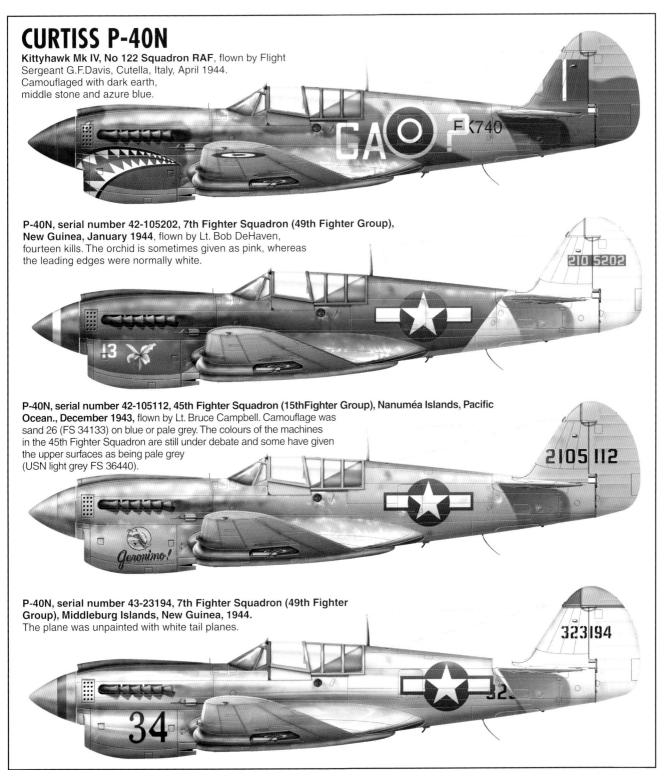

CURTISS P-40N

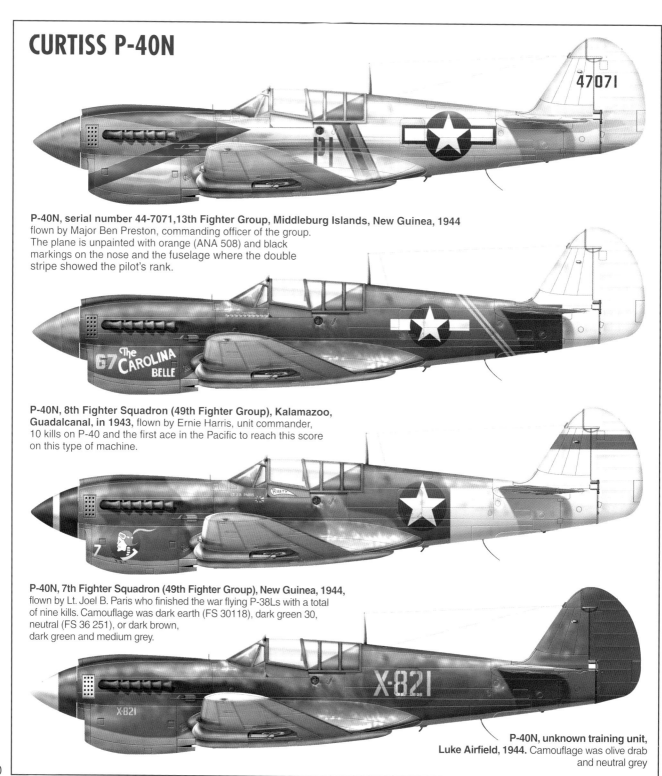

P-40N, serial number 44-7071,13th Fighter Group, Middleburg Islands, New Guinea, 1944
flown by Major Ben Preston, commanding officer of the group.
The plane is unpainted with orange (ANA 508) and black
markings on the nose and the fuselage where the double
stripe showed the pilot's rank.

**P-40N, 8th Fighter Squadron (49th Fighter Group), Kalamazoo,
Guadalcanal, in 1943,** flown by Ernie Harris, unit commander,
10 kills on P-40 and the first ace in the Pacific to reach this score
on this type of machine.

P-40N, 7th Fighter Squadron (49th Fighter Group), New Guinea, 1944,
flown by Lt. Joel B. Paris who finished the war flying P-38Ls with a total
of nine kills. Camouflage was dark earth (FS 30118), dark green 30,
neutral (FS 36 251), or dark brown,
dark green and medium grey.

**P-40N, unknown training unit,
Luke Airfield, 1944.** Camouflage was olive drab
and neutral grey

70

CURTISS P-40N

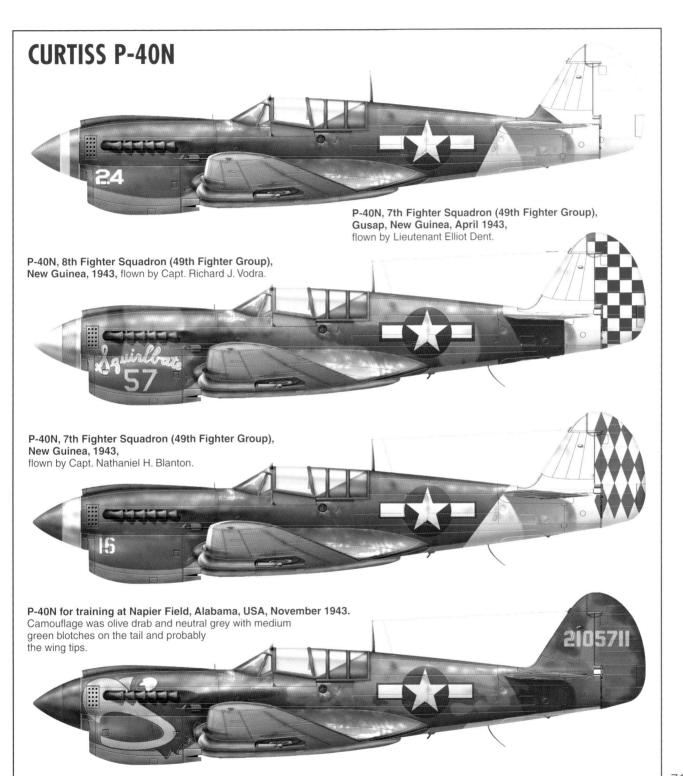

P-40N, 7th Fighter Squadron (49th Fighter Group), Gusap, New Guinea, April 1943, flown by Lieutenant Elliot Dent.

P-40N, 8th Fighter Squadron (49th Fighter Group), New Guinea, 1943, flown by Capt. Richard J. Vodra.

P-40N, 7th Fighter Squadron (49th Fighter Group), New Guinea, 1943, flown by Capt. Nathaniel H. Blanton.

P-40N for training at Napier Field, Alabama, USA, November 1943.
Camouflage was olive drab and neutral grey with medium green blotches on the tail and probably the wing tips.

IN ORDER TO GET BETTER PERFORMANCES...

In order to get better performance, at the beginning of the production run, the P-40F (here the YPF, serial number 41-1602, the third machine produced) was fitted with a radiator between the leading edges prolonged by an aerodynamic fairing. This attempt was intended to reduce air flow problems which caused chronic instability, but it was not followed up. *(USAAC)*

In order to improve visibility and bring it to the same level as that of the P-51D, Curtiss fitted a all-round vision tear-drop canopy, sliding backwards. This installation modified the cross section of the fuselage which was reduced to maintain its line up to the tail. *(USAAC)*

The XP-40K (serial number 42-10219) was another attempt to reduce drag caused by the huge nose air intake, which here was incorporated in the thickness of the leading edges and under the nose. Its opening was completely changed, as was the length of the fuselage, which was identical to the F, whereas the first Ks had a short fuselage (serial numbers 42-45722 to 46321 and 42-9730 to 9929). *(USAFM)*

PROTOTYPES and EXPERIMENTAL MODELS

The XP-40Q During one of the last attempts to improve performance, the XP-40Q, here serial number 42-45722, derived from the P-40K, was fitted with an Allison 1425 bhp V-1710-121 engine and a four-blade propeller. The air intake was reduced, the fuselage was more refined and the wing tips were square. Despite a top speed of 425 mph (680 kph), this model which came out in 1944, ended up being used in civilian post-war races. *(USAF)*

Curtiss XP-60A (serial number 42-79423) and XP-60C (serial number 4279424). These two machines which were the result of the abandoned XP-53 project, represent one of the most radical redesigns of the P-40 airframe. Although it was designed after the D version, the fuselage was completely changed in order for the turbo-charged Allison V1710-75 engine to be installed on the XP-60A which flew for the first time on 1 November 1942. 600 examples were ordered in October 1942, then the order was cancelled in July 1943. The XP-60C flew for the first time in January 1943 with a 2 000 bhp Pratt and Witney R2800-53 engine with contra-rotating airscrews. The results were not conclusive and the plane was modified to accommodate the Packard V-1650-3, thus becoming the XP-60D.

(DR)

(DR) 73

The DIFFERENT VERSIONS of the CURTISS P-40

P-40B/C (designated Curtiss H-81A-2/A-3, Tomahawk Mk IIA/B for the English).
Powerplant: Allison V-1710-33 rated at 1040 bhp.
Armament: Four or six 12.7 mm or 7.7 mm machine guns, depending on the configuration and the models delivered to the English who had a calibre of 7.62 mm.
Some British Tomahawks IIA/B had a Pitot tube on the left wing which was to be found on the machines which were returned to the Flying Tigers in China. There was a ventral pylon for a drop tank.

P-40E (designated Curtiss H-87B-2/H -87A-3/A-4, Kittyhawk Mk I for the English).
Powerplant: Allison V-1710-39 rated at 1150 bhp.
Armament: Six 12.7 mm machine guns, mounted in the wings.
Compared with the P-40B/C, the design of the engine cowling has been changed and the silhouette resembles its final form. Thirty or so P-40Es were eventually sent to the Flying Tigers after a long journey from Africa in mid-1942.

P-40F/F-1 (designated Curtiss H-87D, Kittyhawk Mk II for the English).
Powerplant: Packard V-1650-1 rated at 1300 bhp (a British Rolls-Royce Merlin 28 built under licence.)
Armament: Six 12.7 mm machine guns with the possibility of carrying bombs under the fuselage and the wings.
This version was the first batch of 699 P-40F/F-1s built with the new Packard engine which was recognisable by the absence of the long carburettor air intake over the engine cowling.
The fuselage was not lengthened on these planes and was identical to that of the P-40D/E, i.e. 31 ft 4 ins. Some were fitted with a dorsal fin to improve longitudinal stability, but without success.

P-40F-20 (designated Curtiss H-87D, Kittyhawk Mk II for the English).
Powerplant: Packard V-1650-1 rated at 1300 bhp
Armament: Six 12.7 mm machine guns.
With this variant, from the F-5 until the end of the F-20 production series the fuselage was lengthened by 18 inches by pushing the tail fin back without altering the position of the horizontal surfaces.
his was in order to compensate for low-speed instability. The length was increased to 33 feet. The lower air intake was deeper in order to take the new cooling system.

P-40B/C

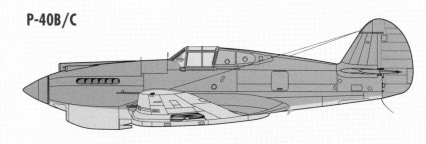

P-40E

P-40F/F-1

P-40F-20

The DIFFERENT VERSIONS of the CURTISS P-40

P-40K-1/K-5

P-40L

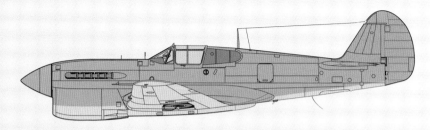

P-40M

P-40N

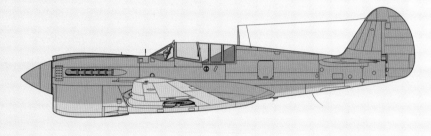

P-40K-1/K-5 (designated Curtiss H-87D, Kittyhawk Mk III for the English).
Powerplant: Allison V-1710-73 rated at 1325 bhp.
Armament: Six 12.7 mm machine guns.
The first 800 built were given a P-40E fuselage, 31 ft 4 ins, with a dorsal fin to compensate for longitudinal instability which had reappeared because of the increased power of the engine. The P-40K-10/K-15s which followed were given the longer fuselage. Note that the chord of the fin was thicker than on the other models. On some models destined for harsh climates, the openings around the exhaust pipes were filled in.

P-40L (designated Curtiss H-87D, Kittyhawk Mk II for the English).
Powerplant: Packard V-1650-1 rated at 1300 bhp.
Armament: Four 12.7 mm machine guns.
In order to reduce weight, the P-40Ls were lightened and two of the wing mounted machine guns were removed. The 50 P-40L-1s built had a standard length fuselage, 31 ft 4 ins, before reverting to the longer one, 33 ft, on the following models P-40L-5 to L-20, as on the model shown here. The long air intake is absent indicating that this plane was fitted with a Packard V-1650-1

P-40M (designated Curtiss H-87D, Kittyhawk Mk III for the English).
Powerplant: Allison V-1710-81 rated at 1200 bhp.
Armament: Six 12.7 mm machine guns.
Apart from its long fuselage inherited from the K-15, the P-40M, which was almost entirely produced for export, had two little panels in front of the exhaust pipes for cooling the engine. One of the other little features of this model was the presence of indicators on the upper wing surfaces to show that the undercarriage was locked in place.

P-40N (designated Curtiss H-87V/W, Kittyhawk Mk IV for the English).
Powerplant: Allison V-1710-81/88/115 rated at between 1 200 and 1360 bhp.
Armament: Four or six 12.7 mm machine guns.
This was the last version to have been produced in large numbers - 5 220 examples. It was also the best performing and one of the lightest versions since some of the original elements had been removed or reworked in lighter materials. From the outside it can be recognised by its longer fuselage, its single-piece canopy without central supports for better sideways and backwards visibility. The P-40M's little grills on the front of the engine cowling were retained.

CURTISS P-40
CAMOUFLAGE SCHEMES
for the MEDITERRANEAN THEATRE
and for the TROPICS

P-40s were painted in various colours ranging from olive drab over neutral grey for the USAAF, with occasional blotches of medium green on the wings and the tail to break up the lines seen from above (particularly the P-40s in the Aleutians), to combinations of dark earth, middle stone, dark earth and light earth, sand, dark green as shown

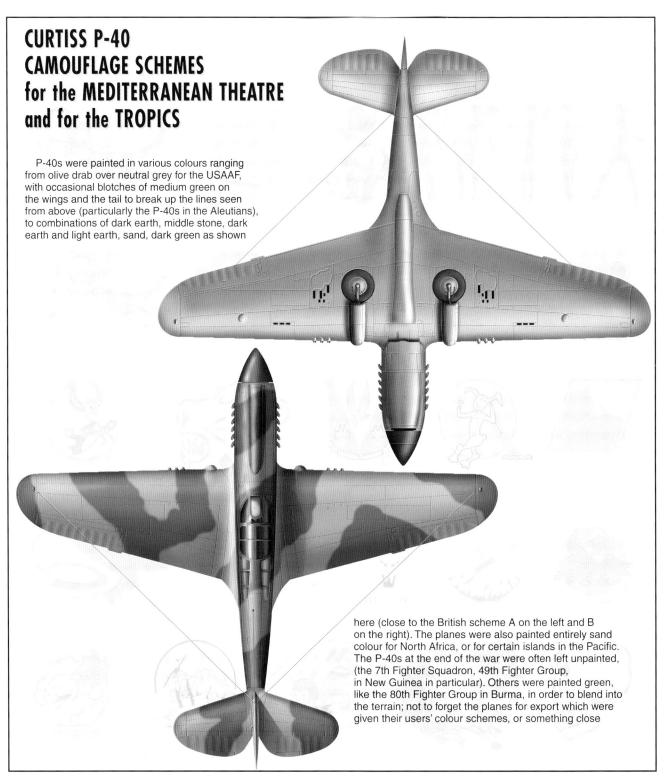

here (close to the British scheme A on the left and B on the right). The planes were also painted entirely sand colour for North Africa, or for certain islands in the Pacific. The P-40s at the end of the war were often left unpainted, (the 7th Fighter Squadron, 49th Fighter Group, in New Guinea in particular). Others were painted green, like the 80th Fighter Group in Burma, in order to blend into the terrain; not to forget the planes for export which were given their users' colour schemes, or something close

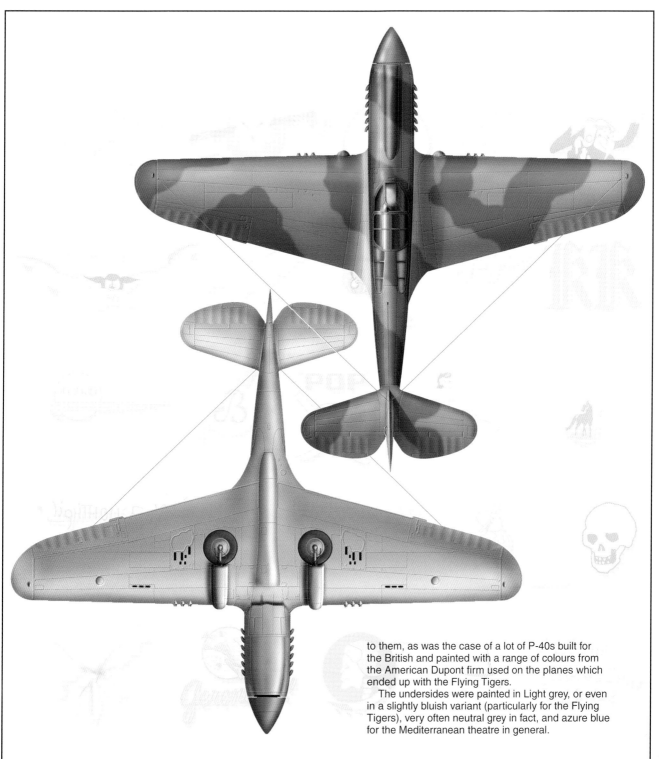

to them, as was the case of a lot of P-40s built for the British and painted with a range of colours from the American Dupont firm used on the planes which ended up with the Flying Tigers.

The undersides were painted in Light grey, or even in a slightly bluish variant (particularly for the Flying Tigers), very often neutral grey in fact, and azure blue for the Mediterranean theatre in general.

The RANGE of LOADS CARRIED
by the CURTISS P-40

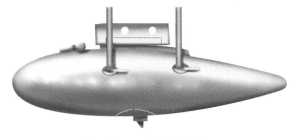

52-gallon tank (196.6 l).

500 lb bomb (227 kg)

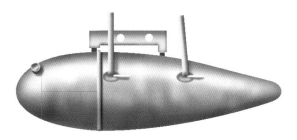

52-gallon tank

500 lb bomb

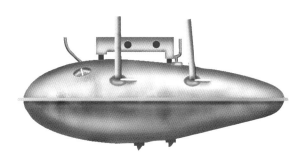

52-gallon tank

British 250 lb bomb (113.5 kg)

1 000lb bomb (454 kg)

50 lb bomb (22.7 kg)

FLYING TIGERS MARKINGS

Insignia of the 1st Pursuit Squadron, 'Adam and Eve'
The planes in this unit whose tail stripe was white,
were numbered from 1 to 33.

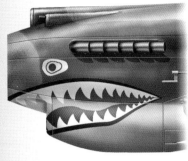

Insignia of the 2nd Pursuit Squadron. The batch assigned to this
squadron was numbered 34 to 66. The tail stripe was blue.
This unit also had a distinctive emblem: a little black and white panda.

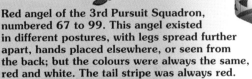

Red angel of the 3rd Pursuit Squadron,
numbered 67 to 99. This angel existed
in different postures, with legs spread further
apart, hands placed elsewhere, or seen from
the back; but the colours were always the same,
red and white. The tail stripe was always red.

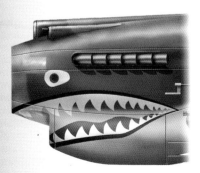

*NB. In order to identify the Flying Tigers' P-40B/Cs, it is better to check the tail stripe
rather than their numbering as many machines were transferred from one unit
to another during their time in China.*

CURTISS P-40B/C of the FLYING TIGERS

Thanks to all the different versions in the different scales — from the 1/32nd Revell P-40 E, the numerous 1/72nd models (Airfix/Heller, Frog, Aademy, Hasegawa, etc) to the 1/48th Revell and Monogram (whose P-40B is probably the best of them all because of the accuracy of its dimensions) — there has been a P-40 revival.

Let us start however with the Otaki model which came out a good twenty years ago. It was quite a good rendition at 1/48th, etched but with rather heavy riveting. Hobbycraft took up the model recently. Next were the Revell/Monogram 1/48th models, brought out again in the middle of the nineties in the Promodeler range and slightly

Among the more interesting P-40 decorations are naturally those worn by the P-40B/C Tomahawks of the Flying Tigers. The model represents Bill Reed's '75' white, recognisable by its characteristic red angel.

The left side of the plane shows signs of wear and is covered with dust and various spillages. The decals are well caught between two layers of gloss varnish, then covered with a matt base which allows no over-thickness, so that they then blend well into the colours of the camouflage.

remoulded; the Japanese Mauve kits (P-40M/N), fine, relatively accurate but whose detailing left a little to be desired; and the very nice series of P-40F/K/Ns, from AMT - nowadays a very hard-to-find make -whose models featured softer plastic, fine etching and sophisticated finishing. At the same scale, it was a pleasure to discover a new American producer, AmTech's P-40 E - the ex-AMT/ERTL model which had never been brought out; and a P-40M from Eduard, which has brought out the Mauve kit but with a host of resin details and a very nice sheet of decals. At the time of writing, other models ought to be seeing the light of day, coming from the USA and covering rather rarer versions like the P-40F and L.

For the 1/72 modelers, the Japanese firm Hasegawa has brought out the best moulds of the P-40 E and N. Also at this scale there are the P-40F/Ms from MPM and Kovozavody (Czech producers), quite well turned out but rather cruder; from Academy, a quality Korean producer; the new P-40B from Pavla another Czech maker, in a limited edition and needing good attention to the parts and therefore destined for the experienced model-maker; and a P-40Q from Pegasus, the English maker whose products are intended for the same public.

In the 1/32nd range, there is the Revell model already mentioned, but also a P-40B/C from the American firm Craftwork, all in resin. It is quite good and the only model of this version at this scale, though rather difficult to build.

The Academy kit presented here (taking up the old Hobbycraft model) is not the definitive model of the P-40B/C, as the general form is a bit doubtful, but it is good when compared to the amount of detailing needed on the Monogram version (re-etching, improving the cockpit). The accessory sheets brought out by Part, a Polish accessory maker (ref. 48 073/76/77) will enable the modeler to produce something reasonable while waiting for the introduction of something better along more modern standards.

This kit has already dealt with in great detail in Wing Masters N°26 together with a historical article about the Flying Tigers; it is painted with Gunze acrylic paint and decorated with one of the new sheets from Eagle Cals (ref. EC.32), in the colours of the plane flown by Bill Reed of the 3rd Pursuit Squadron (serial P-8186)

Detail painting and assembly: Julien Haccoun
Camouflage and decoration: Anis el Bied.

Photo-etched kits from Part enable the landing flaps with all the internal details to be shown in the down position.

The new Chinese roundels are placed just overlapping the original British markings: this was one of the features of this plane. The camouflage is painted on using stencils, as in the factory, before the plane, originally destined for the RAF was delivered.

BIBLIOGRAPHY

MAGAZINES

— *Wings Of Fame*, Vol. 9: « *American Volunteer Group, History of the US Volunteer fighters in China, the famous Flying Tigers* »,
  Robert F. Dorr, Aerospace Publishing, 1997.
— *MPM* n°96, juillet-août 1979.
— *Wing Masters* n° 11, juillet-août 1999.
— *Euro Modelismo* n° 83, juin 1999.
— *Le Fanatique de l'Aviation* n° 130 à 145 et 288.

BOOKS

— **American Volunteer Group Colours and Markings**, Terrill Clements, Osprey, 2001.
— **P-40 Warhawks Aces of the MTO**, Carl Malesworth, Osprey, 2002.
— **P-40 Warhawk Aces of the CBI**, Carl Molesworth, Osprey, 2002.
— **Walk Around P-40 Warhawk**, Vol. 8, Lou Drendel, Squadron Signal Publications, 1996.
— **Tigers Over China, The Aircraft of the AVG**, Thomas A. Tullis, Eagle Editions LTD, 2001
— **Fighters of World War II**, Charles W. Cain & Mike Jerram, Profile Publications LTD., 1979.
— **P-40 Warhawk in World War II Color**, Jeffrey Ethell, Motorbooks International, 1994.
— **The 79th Fighter Group Over Tunisia, Sicily and Italy in World War II**, Don Woerpel, Schiffer, 2001.
— **P-40 Warhawk, Vol. 61, Detail & Scale**, Bert Kinzey, Squadron Signal Publications, 1999.
— **P-40 Warhawk, Vol. 62, Detail & Scale**, Bert Kinzey, Squadron Signal Publications, 1999.
— **Curtiss P-40**, Vlastimil Ehrman, Valerij Roman, MBI, 1998.
— **Combat Colours Number 3, The Curtiss P-36 and P-40 in USAAC/USAAF service 1939 to 1945**, H.C. Bridgwater, Guideline Publications, 2001.
— **49th Fighter Group**, Ernest R. McDowell, Squadron Signal Publications, 1989.
— **Curtiss P-40 in Action** n°26, Ernest Mc Dowell, Squadron Signal Publications, 1976.
— **Air Force Colors, Vol. 3**, Pacific and Home front, 1942-1947, Dana Bell, Squadron Signal Publications, 1997.
— **Combat Colours** n° 4, Pearl Harbour and beyond, December 1941 to May 1942.
— **USAAF Fighters Units MTO, 1942-45**, Christopher Shores, Aircam Air War n°12, Osprey, 1978.
— **Aces of the Southwest Pacific**, Gene B. Stafford, Squadron Signal Publications, 1977.
— **Checkertails, the 325th Fighter Group in the Second World War**, Ernest McDowell, Squadron Signal Publications, 1994.

MISCELLANEOUS

— *Connaissance de l'Histoire* n° 53, Hachette, février 1983.
— *Fanatique de l'Aviation*, Hors Série n°15 « l'Armée de l'Air dans la Deuxième Guerre mondiale ».
— *Famous Airplanes of the World*, Burin Do n° 117, janvier 1980.
— *Mach 1, l'Encyclopédie de l'Aviation*, n° 37, 42, 48. Atlas.

AKNOWLEDGEMENTS

We should like to thank *Jean-François Micheletti*, *Denis Gillé*, *Julien Haccou*n and *Vincent Gréciet* for their help in the realisation of this book and for making all their documentation available to us.

Design and Lay-out by Daniel LAURELUT and Yann-Erwin ROBERT, © *Histoire & Collections 2002*.

Un ouvrage édité par
HISTOIRE & COLLECTIONS
SA au capital de 182 938, 82 €

5, avenue de la République
F-75541 Paris Cédex 11
Téléphone: 01 40 21 18 20
Fax: 01 47 00 51 11

This book has been designed, typed, laid-out and processed by *'Le studio graphique Armes & Collections'* fully integrated computer equipment.

Printed by Zure
Spain, European Union
December 2002